BLOOD ON THE SUN

*Also by Chad Merriman
in Large Print:*

The Avengers

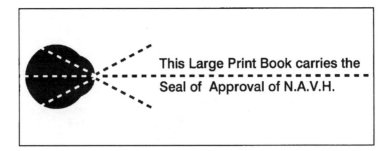

This Large Print Book carries the
Seal of Approval of N.A.V.H.

BLOOD ON THE SUN

Chad Merriman

WHEELER
PUBLISHING

Lg Pt
MER

Published in 2004 by arrangement with
Golden West Literary Agency.

Wheeler Large Print Western.

The text of this Large Print edition is unabridged.
Other aspects of the book may vary from the original edition.

Set in 16 pt. Plantin by Ramona Watson.

Printed in the United States on permanent paper.

Library of Congress Cataloging-in-Publication Data

Merriman, Chad.
    Blood on the sun / Chad Merriman.
       p. cm.
    ISBN 1-58724-792-5 (lg. print : sc : alk. paper)
    1. Overland journeys to the Pacific — Fiction.
2. Women pioneers — Fiction.   3. Indian women —
Fiction.   4. Wagon trains — Fiction.   5. Large type books.
I. Title.
PS3553.H38B59 2004
813'.54—dc22   2004054448

As the Founder/CEO of NAVH, the only national health agency solely devoted to those who, although not totally blind, have an eye disease which could lead to serious visual impairment, I am pleased to recognize Thorndike Press* as one of the leading publishers in the large print field.

Founded in 1954 in San Francisco to prepare large print textbooks for partially seeing children, NAVH became the pioneer and standard setting agency in the preparation of large type.

Today, those publishers who meet our standards carry the prestigious "Seal of Approval" indicating high quality large print. We are delighted that Thorndike Press is one of the publishers whose titles meet these standards. We are also pleased to recognize the significant contribution Thorndike Press is making in this important and growing field.

Lorraine H. Marchi, L.H.D.
Founder/CEO
NAVH

* Thorndike Press encompasses the following imprints: Thorndike, Wheeler, Walker and Large Print Press.

CHAPTER ONE

Starbright made camp where a branch of the Platte slid under tall and tawny bluffs. The stream brawled lustily, breaking up the mountain quiet. Sheltering cottonwood lined the eroded banks, with grass plentiful on a flat between the water and a hill. It was an excellent campsite, yet Dix Starbright was scowling.

A while ago he had seen the stretched-out tags of white that meant a passing wagon train of emigrants, out on the edge of the prairie. Afterward he had seen stragglers, three wagons a few miles behind the main caravan. Something had stalled the laggard wagons. The oxen were unyoked, and Starbright had seen the smoke of a camp-fire.

The sight had reminded him that earlier he had seen Sioux drifting out of the hills. They had not been warriors but a mixture of bucks, squaws, and children. Starbright had thought they were moving down to the train in hopes of gifts, perhaps a feast. Yet the lone wagon stood in danger from that party, and so Starbright was pitching camp in this recess, unknown to the stragglers.

A buckskin man, he was sympathetic with his own white race, yet his years in the Rocky Mountain fur trade had also made him feel akin to the Indians, and he understood the compulsions driving them, too.

Starbright unsaddled, dropping the empty packs of his five Indian ponies. He necklooped and picketed the tough little animals on the grass. A glance through the matted tops of the cottonwoods showed a fiery sun dropping behind the Laramies. The dying light changed the river's yellow to bloody red. The bare earth where Starbright stood was now stained copper. The sterile river bluffs gave off a flaming yellow of their own.

These effects were gone by the time Starbright had cooked supper. Night wheeled in upon his camp so quickly that the blaze of the fire against the obscure mass of foliage was a comfort to him.

A tall and tapering man of unusual size, he wore nothing but buckskin, except for his beaver cap. His hair, a ropey yellow, tumbled to hard-fleshed shoulders. A rusty stand of beard had accumulated during his six weeks on the trail. He had left Fort Laramie with ten packs of trade goods, and he was now heading in without a single fur taken from the Indians in exchange. He had distributed the goods as gifts, a mark of appreciation and his farewell to the Indians. He had smoked a last friendly pipe in a hundred scattered lodges. Tonight would be his final lonely camp on the prairie. He savored it as he rolled up in his blankets.

Lost in reminiscence and eagerness for the change ahead, he was startled by the burst of gunshots which came muffled through the night, helped along by the mountain breeze. He was on his feet instantly, kicking aside his blankets and remembering the straggling settler wagons. He thrust his two pistols under the buckskin band of his pants and caught up bullet pouch and powder horn.

A few long strides took him to the closest pony. He threw off the neck rope, leaped to its bare back and drove it forward, guiding it by his knees. The little mustang gave out with a nervous burst of speed.

The dark night kept the stragglers' camp hidden until Starbright was nearly upon it. Forward a campfire sprang into being against the backdrop of a high bench. The light revealed only one of the big prairie schooners; its size seemed to Starbright to be extraordinary. The oxen had moved to the grass. Starbright, coming closer, saw three horses at the camp. He discerned the shapes of people lined against the big wagon, their hands held high.

In the same moment the quiet was cut by ribbons of fire and the air was rocked by pistol shots. Instinctively Starbright kneed his mount on a sharp quarter, hearing the searching whine of a bullet. He had pulled both pistols but he didn't shoot because of the settlers against the wagon.

He was bewildered because the pattern dealt the Sioux out of this. He kept quartering, watching the winking, red streaks of death.

"Get around 'em, men!" he bawled in his booming, great voice, as if to confederates. "There are only three of them!"

He was certain now that he confronted a trio of white renegades. He flung two shots, shooting high because of the settlers, and kept driving toward the wagons.

He saw shapes climb into saddles. Three riders whipped out, cutting along under the rim. They rode heedlessly, twisting in the saddle to fling more shots back at Starbright. He made a quick decision and swung his pony around in pursuit. Excitement boiled in him as he enjoyed the success of his trick.

Starbright's string of ponies had been carefully selected. He gained on the three, clinging to a heedless gait that at any moment could have spilled and killed him. He was crowding them hard, and this was his weapon against them.

The men ahead had stopped shooting and now bent their efforts to escape. Suddenly one of the harried horses tangled on the rough underfooting. Starbright saw it go headlong, its hind quarters coming up and over as it crashed. The other two riders never slacked speed. The spilled horse staggered up and went on, unsteady, riderless.

Starbright pulled up at the still figure of a man on the ground. He stood warily, ready for trouble. But the man's head was twisted too far around to look right. Even before he bent to investigate, Starbright decided that his neck was broken. The mountain man squatted on his moccasined heels, the escaped riders almost out of hearing.

This man did not wear buckskin but the homespun of the settler breed. Shaking his head puzzledly, Starbright swung the body across a big shoulder. The pony followed obediently as he started back toward the wagon camp.

He called out reassuringly as he came close. The nearing firelight showed him stirring figures. At first he thought that they mistrusted and meant to drive him off. He tramped up to the campfire, the pony at his heels like a faithful dog.

Still holding the body he had brought in, Starbright stared into the eyes of a tall girl. She wore a nightgown, and her black hair was in braids that crossed her shoulders to fall before firm breasts. He saw her attention sweep him from moccasins to shaggy

11

head. Her eyes showed something that was either appreciation or amusement. Her lips parted over gleaming teeth.

"A one-man cavalry troop!" she murmured.

"Are you alone?" a man's voice asked.

Starbright shot his glance to the speaker. He saw a tall, thin man wearing what Starbright remembered was called a night-shirt. He had a shock of iron-gray hair and wore a mustache.

There were four other men in the fringes of the firelight. These were more like the settler breed, land-hungry farmers heading for the Oregon country.

Starbright placed his burden on the ground, saying, "Know him?"

The men of the wagon party pressed closer. They stared down at the dead renegade, whom the light disclosed to be a young, swart man like a thousand others from the Missouri River settlements. The fellow had worn a black handkerchief over his face, but he had pulled it off in his flight and it now hung about that grotesquely loosened neck.

"Anybody recognize him?" Starlight repeated.

He saw heads shake all about him. Nobody spoke up in identification.

In a half-angry voice, Starbright said, "I can tell you he's not a local product. He's from the main train, or else they followed you."

"How do you know that?" the girl asked.

"His duds. And his looks. I know the mountain population. My name's Starbright, and I been trading out of Fort Laramie a long while."

That information seemed to ease the party. The tall man in the nightshirt smiled for the first time.

"We're obliged, Starbright," he said. "My name's Kelly Lang. These three wagons are traveling together, though we're attached to the train you must have seen. One of our wagons had trouble with a wheel and we dropped back to fix it. We'll catch up tomorrow. We're bound for the Willamette settlements." As an afterthought, he looked at the girl and added, "My daughter, Rita."

Starbright tipped his head, frowning. "Didn't you have a guard posted? This is Sioux country, man. They've been watching your wagons for days."

"We had a guard," Lang said, "but the bandits came in shooting. They were on us before we knew it. I have no idea what they were after."

"Food, whisky, ammunition," said Starbright, still scowling at the girl. "Or it could be they'd caught sight of the pretty lady." He didn't like the amusement that kept haunting her features. Yet she was very attractive in her thin gown.

"Well, we won't be come upon so easily a

second time," Lang promised.

Starbright nodded at the dead man and said, "Bury him." He turned toward his pony, went up to its back and rode off without farewell. . . .

Morning found Starbright back on the trail. He was again upon the prairie with its high verdure of sage, rabbit brush, and gramma grass. As a speck against that vegetation, he could discern the shapes of buildings he knew to be the trading post of Sam Hack, a free trapper. The dots enlarged and took shape as Starbright drew nearer to make his last call before returning to Fort Laramie.

Two small log buildings faced each other. Along one side ran the sharp uprights of an unfinished stockade. An Indian lodge stood in the farther distance, and dogs cut loose and rushed at Starbright in a sudden noisy welcome.

A man came out of one of the cabins as Starbright neared, a buckskin man with tousled gray hair, yawning widely. His heavy jaws snapped shut when he recognized the visitor.

"Damn your eyes, Dix!" Sam Hack boomed. "Old Broken Knee was here, yestiday. Said you'd kited your tail." Hack snapped a string of curses at the yapping dogs, silencing them.

"Getting set for that, Sam," Starbright

agreed, sliding from the saddle. He offered his hand and it was caught in a crushing grip.

Hack's gray mane was curly. Like Starbright's, it reached his shoulders. He wore a fancy buckskin shirt, embroidered with dyed porcupine quills by his squaw. He was a squat man, wide at the shoulders, with thick, stubby legs encased like sausages in greasy, campblackened leggings. Turning, Hack clapped his hands together.

His Indian wife, who had been peering through the doorway, stepped forth, three children spilling out after her. At Hack's unintelligible grunt, the squaw took the reins of Starbright's horse.

"Water," Starbright told her. "But don't unsaddle. I got to get on."

"Why in holy hell you going to Oregon?" Hack demanded.

Starbright frowned. "What's left here, Sam? The fur trade's done for. You men with families have got something to stay for. I ain't." He knew that Hack did not have to be told of the ruin of the fur trade. It was the talk wherever trappers and fur traders met on the trails. The beaver were thinning out, but that wasn't the main trouble. Men in the East had turned against beaver hats, switching to silk stovepipes. Skins no longer brought price enough to make the fur trade the booming industry it had been for so long.

"Your own fault you ain't got a family, too," Hack said. "You could have had any Injun gal in the high country. Even princesses. Way you've dodged their lodges is a disgrace to your buckskins. Well, come in, man. I got news." The trader led the way into his living quarters.

Following, Starbright found himself in a smelly room of a type he knew well. It was a small square, a fire blazing even in this summer season. The smoke escaped through a hole in the roof ridge. Except for buffalo hides and Indian paraphernalia scattered about, there were no furnishings. Hack's rifle stood by the door, and Starbright observed Indian bows and deerskin quivers of arrows.

Two bucks sat by the fire, cross-legged and unmoving. Starbright knew them to be relatives of Hack's squaw. They looked up at Starbright with the blank hostility that was the mark of their tribe. Starbright stared back in the same fierce way, knowing they would respect nothing less than a full return of their attitude. They were Sioux, the most quarrelsome nation in the high country.

The white men seated themselves in the manner of the braves, but across the fire from them.

"See the wagon company down the river?" Hack asked.

"Saw them," Starbright answered.

"If you figure on going to Oregon," drawled Hack, "you better not latch onto it. You wouldn't like your captain a'tall."

"Packing alone," Starbright said. "Like my own company."

"Go ahead and spoil my surprise," said Hack. "Don't ask who the captain is."

"I know him?"

"Ought to."

"All right. Who is it?"

Hack grinned. "Man named Redburn."

"Not Tyre Redburn!" Starbright sucked in a noisy breath. His eyes widened and grew fierce in their intensity as they stared at the squat trader. "Sure of it, Sam? Redburn wouldn't dare come back here. Not even alone, much less to lead a wagon train through the high country."

"Dare or not, he's here." Hack nodded toward the two Sioux. "They went down with some others, last night, to visit the train. Got no welcome a'tall from Tyre Redburn. No wonder. That jack-a-dandy stands to get his hair lifted afore he gets to the pass. And his company butchered."

"Guess he's the kind of fool that would try it," Starbright admitted. "He's crazy."

"Ain't he?" Hack asked. "Them settlers don't know what they're in for. Ten to one the words already reached Walking Crow that Redburn's back. If so, them wagons won't reach the Sweetwater, even."

Starbright noted the gleam in the eyes of the two Sioux across the fire. They understood a little English. They were hurt at the rebuff suffered when they had tried to visit Redburn's wagon train. But feelings deeper than that had been aroused in them. They were not members of Walking Crow's own village, but one motive that could put down tribal hostilities and unite the Indians was their hatred of the white settlers. The trappers and traders they tolerated, even grew to like, since they benefited by the fur trade. But nothing but ruin could ever come from the settlers.

Hack looked at Starbright a long moment and added, "How about you, Dix? You were close to The Pheasant. I recollect your face wasn't good to look at when it come out about her and Tyre Redburn."

"I'll figure out about me if I run into Redburn," Starbright retorted. For a moment his mind was filled by the picture of the Indian princess called The Pheasant, daughter of one of the Sioux's most truculent tribal chiefs. She had been a beautiful wildling with a child's emotions and the body of a devastating woman. Starbright himself had wanted her, could have had her in his tepee. It hadn't been easy for him to pass by the delight she would have so freely given him. Then along had come Tyre Redburn, a gentleman adventurer with an entirely dif-

18

ferent code of personal conduct.

Hack's squaw came in then, and the two bucks licked their lips. A visitor always meant food and a smoke. Hack used white man's coffee, which made his post an attraction for miles around. Starbright shared the steaming coffee and the common pipe. Afterward he distributed the last of his presents.

The reserve, which had to be broken down at each encounter, gradually left the Indian men. They shook hands all around in farewell. Starbright had always been the type of trader who could ride any trail without having to watch his back.

He was ready now for the much longer trail to the Willamette Valley.

CHAPTER TWO

Empty hills closed in ahead of him. He topped them to see below another stream that poured into the Platte. This was the Laramie. Finally he sighted the high clay walls of Fort Laramie itself, set upon a rise beyond the stream and against a marching line of naked ridges.

Riding on through the sage, Starbright reached a ford and crossed over. Afterward he traversed a sagebrush flat, dropped down into a hollow, then climbed out again at the gateway of the fort.

Half a dozen mountain men stood watching. Then Starbright was laughing and shaking hands all about, with Lamont, the bourgeois, and Fallon, Beauville, and Trestrois. They were French Canadians on a summer holiday. Old Dukehart, in Starbright's absence, had brought his trading wagons in from the Niobrara. Devine, Ellsworth, and Lafferty, American trappers, were there also — all strapping men of the high mountains, as excited as children by the small change in the day's dull routine.

"Dix done what he claimed!" bawled

Devine. "He went out with full packs and gave it all away. Man's crazy!"

"Goin' to Oregon, ain't he?" Ellsworth said in his sleepy drawl. "That's crazy country and a crazy notion. So givin' away ten packs of goods is right in Dix's line. Ike, fetch a shovel. I know where old Trestrois planted a jug."

"Dig heem up," Trestrois said cheerfully. "Save me the work."

Starbright grinned and shook his head. "Have to skip the fiesta, boys. Wagon train's on its way. White women. So we got to act like gentlemen, like it or not."

"Not like white women?" Lafferty asked. The trappers looked at each other, the jug forgotten. Once the year's high point had been the annual rendezvous with the fur-company wagons from St. Louis. Now it was the emigration through each summer, the big trains of settler wagons bound for the Far West. Great numbers of white women traveled with them. The trappers expected nothing from them but the pleasure of seeing them. They confined their more virile efforts to the native daughters. Now Lafferty, an aggressive Irishman, let out a whoop and headed for the fort's corrals and a horse to ride out and meet the wagons. He started a general exodus.

Laughing, Starbright led his own animals to the fort's mud-walled corrals. Returning

21

from the corrals, Starbright struck off across the central compound. It was walled, and the thick adobe was buttressed by the backs of log buildings arranged about an inner square. Standing about and even basking on the roofs were Indian bucks, connected with the fort through squaws taken by the trappers and traders. Mixed children darted and whooped. White *engages* were at work in the shops, the racket of their industry mixing with the general tumult. Starbright crossed the compound and climbed a pair of stairs to a crude and snaking balcony. A row of doors ran before him, opening into the rooms of the single men. The flat roofs of these structures served as a banquette for the defense of the fort's walls.

Opening a door, Starbright stepped into the cubicle that long had been his closest approach to a home. He wrinkled his nose and left the door ajar to release the room's trapped smells. There was a rough bunk filled with mashed straw, some buffalo robes at its foot. A chair, a dresser, and an empty water pail completed the room's furnishings. A buck had brought up Starbright's saddlebags and bedroll. They had been dumped in the middle of the floor.

Starbright cursed the empty water bucket and went back to the well to fill it. Then he shaved himself before one of his trading mirrors, scrubbed himself, and donned clean buckskins. His relaxed mind began to toy again with the incident of the night before. It was stretching the imagination too far to suppose that the three thieves had drifted this far west of the Missouri River in search of easy plunder.

It was logical enough that three straggling wagons had been an open invitation to thieves. The odd thing was their being in the area at all if they weren't part of the wagon company. It would take a strong pull to bring homespun men into Sioux country in so small a party. It must have been some attraction in the caravan, possibly in the straggler party. Starbright, in retrospect, had grown less sure that Kelly Lang had told the truth. Before Starbright's arrival, the ruffians had been there long enough to have demanded what they wanted. Certainly the party he had helped out of trouble had not been honest with him.

Moreover, a new element had been introduced into that situation by what Sam Hack had revealed. Tyre Redburn, leading the train, must have realized the sheer folly of three lone wagons falling back so far, particularly for an overnight camp. As captain, he would have had to consent to the fallback. Redburn was a crazy fool when it came to personal daring, but it seemed illogical that he would have been so careless with his charges.

The supper bell rang out while Starbright was smoking his pipe. Protocol was strict at Laramie. As a free trader, Starbright ate with the bourgeois and principal *engages*. It was a plain meal of dried meat and bread. Later the hunters and trappers would eat here, while the Indians and white derelicts taken in by the fort would take the leavings apart from their betters. Starbright had never liked the class distinction but knew it was even stricter in the Hudson's Bay Company establishments.

He emerged from the dining hall to notice a rustle of excitement at the main gate. Starbright walked forward and found a half-dozen men standing outside the gate, all staring off toward the dusk-mantled river.

The hills beyond the river showed a throng of oncoming Indians moving down upon the Laramie. They were Sioux and, like the Indians Starbright had seen earlier, they must have been attracted by the approaching line of wagons. It was a whole village, Starbright saw, coming to the fort to mingle and trade with the emigrants.

Dogs darted about. Tired ponies trudged forward under the burden of heavy travois. The procession came to the river on a wide front and without pause began to splash across.

"Cuss my kin!" a trapper shouted. "It's Walking Crow's whole village."

"Walking Crow?" Starbright said sharply.

A bolt of apprehension hit him. He had said nothing here at the fort of Tyre Redburn's return to the high country as leader of the oncoming train. But it was not a coincidence that Walking Crow was arriving here at this time for news traveled swiftly over the Indian grapevine. The Sioux chief knew that Tyre Redburn was back. This arrival of his entire village meant trouble.

Starbright sought out Lamont and belatedly reported the information.

"Redburn?" gasped Lamont. "Dix, it isn't possible. No man's that crazy."

"Redburn is," Starbright drawled. "A couple of Hack's in-laws saw him leading that train. Walking Crow's come down to get even for the little trick Redburn played on him. He's here to avenge the death of The Pheasant."

Lamont threw his hands upward. "Why don't he go and massacree them, then, and not bother us?"

"You know what happened," Starbright resumed. "Walking Crow will do it his own way. That will be as hard on Redburn as he can make it. A lot of people think the Sioux have no feelings. But Walking Crow was plain crazy about his girl. The Pheasant wasn't only a little beauty — she had a heart full of love for everybody. Out of all the trappers in these hills, Redburn was the only one who'd take advantage of that."

"If he's come here after Redburn, he'd only laugh if I asked him to leave. Dix, you go stop that train. I'll give Walking Crow presents and a feast. Tomorrow, maybe, he'll go back to Buffalo Creek."

"He won't," said Starbright. "But I'll try. I've got to." He took the first horse he could rope out of the corral and swung up bareback. None of the trappers who had gone out to meet the wagons had come back, which was evidence that the train was coming on to the fort before it camped.

Starbright swung down the river to cross, avoiding the Indians now making camp on the flat. Thereafter he cut cross country to the emigrant trail that followed the river. Dusk deepened, and the lonely sounds of the wasteland came to him. The country rose and fell beneath the hoofs of his horse.

He came upon the train closer to the fort than he liked. Starbright saw the vague shapes coming along the trail soon after he heard the rumbled warning through the twilight. He waved down the pilot wagons, oxen outfits plodding wearily forward. To a man with a bullwhack Starbright called, "Where's your captain?" The man replied by jerking a thumb tiredly over his shoulder.

Starbright rode on, watching wagons down the line come to a halt as the forward vehicles blocked the way. Another rider

26

came along the stretched-out train, picking up speed. He sat his horse like an Indian or a mountain man, but he wore eastern clothing. Yet Starbright would have recognized Tyre Redburn by his size alone or the confident way he carried his broad shoulders and handsome head.

"Did you stop this train?" Redburn called. "What's wrong?"

"I stopped it, Tyre," Starbright agreed. There was an oversized wagon just off to his left, obscured by the growing night. So the Lang party had rejoined the train. He sat there, waiting.

Redburn rode on up, studying him. He gasped, "Dix Starbright! I heard you were still at the fort. Some of the boys came out and got themselves adopted by my people. They're shining up to our girls. But why are you here, Dix? As I remember, you never cared much for that kind of fun." His voice was smooth, cultivated, taunting.

Tyre Redburn was a big man, as large as Starbright. He had no capacity for fear, Starbright knew. When he showed caution it was in the way of a gambler weighing the chances and plunging or withdrawing according to the advantages for himself. When he saw an opening he wanted, Redburn would go through it at any cost. Starbright knew it would be hard to handle him now.

"Something happened at the fort after Lafferty and the boys left," Starbright said. "Walking Crow came in with his whole village. You remember him, don't you, Redburn? He ain't been visiting us since you left these parts so sudden. He's come a long piece from Buffalo Creek. He knows you're coming."

"Walking Crow?" Redburn said in a sharp, quick way. He glanced uneasily at the big wagon and lowered his voice. "Well, we had a visit from a Sioux hunting party a few days ago. I thought it would reach Walking Crow that I'm back. But I didn't expect trouble until we hit his part of the country. That's days ahead yet."

"Looks like he's anxious to greet you," Starbright drawled. He wanted to persuade the man so he lowered his own voice accommodatingly. "You better make camp here. Lamont's going to butter the chief with a feast and gifts. He'll try to get him to leave in the morning."

"The devil with that, Starbright." Redburn had recovered from his initial surprise and his voice, though still quiet, was easy. "I told these people we'd camp tonight at Laramie. That's where we'll do it."

"Tell 'em about Walking Crow, too?" murmured Starbright. "That you're apt to find yourself castrated if you come too close to him?"

"Why should I?" Redburn asked, his voice roughening.

"Make camp, or I'll tell 'em the bald facts and without trimmings." He lifted his voice loud enough so that it could be heard at the wagons.

Redburn shot another quick look at the oversized vehicle. He said, "Damn you, Starbright. All right." He spurred his horse ahead.

Starbright waited, holding down his own heated mount. He had figured that Redburn might be more afraid of being found out by these people than he was of the Sioux. Yet most men would have been terrified by the threat Walking Crow now posed. A chief might share his wives with friends and guests, but his daughters were a different proposition. Anyone foolish enough to take one without proper arrangements with her father had trouble on his hands, the fullest cruelty of which the Sioux were capable.

Yet it had been and still was Starbright's opinion that this flavoring of high danger had made The Pheasant all the more attractive to Tyre Redburn.

The voice that called to Starbright was a woman's and came from the vagueness of the big wagon.

"Why did you stop us?" she asked. "What's this about bald facts?"

A thrill shot through Starbright. The

29

speaker was Rita Lang, who must have heard bits of the exchange with Redburn. So she was the main reason the man had knuckled down so swiftly when threatened. Tyre Redburn had a fierce appetite for women. It stood to reason he had found at least one to his liking in this big train. Starbright rode in.

The wagon's driver leaned wearily against a wheel and gave a jaded nod at Starbright. The girl looked down from the seat under the front bow of the canvas top. Starbright touched his cap, staring up at her. She was dressed now, and he could see her slender upper body outlined against the sky, her bare, smooth head, the full suggestion of her breasts under her dress.

"You?" she breathed suddenly. "What are you saving us from this time, Dix Starbright?"

So she had remembered his name. That took some of the sting out of her tart question. "Don't give two hoots in hell," Starbright exploded, "what happens to you personally. But there's others in this train I wouldn't want to see scalped. Some Indians showed up at Fort Laramie this evening wouldn't be healthy for you to mix with. So I persuaded your captain to camp here for tonight."

"We've met Indians more than once!" Rita retorted, a sudden temper coming into her voice. "They just beg and strut. We've had no trouble."

"These might correct your notion," Starbright answered. "Anyhow, your captain seems to figure so. Looks like you're making camp."

"I expect our captain knows this country as well as you do," Rita rejoined.

So she knew Redburn's history, or part of it.

The leading wagons had started turning. Riding forward, Starbright saw them being pulled into a circle on the river flat. He let his horse jog on and presently came upon Redburn, who sat a motionless mount.

In a sterner voice Redburn said, "I went along with you, Starbright, and against my will. I'm hoping you kept your mouth shut."

Starbright laughed. "She the one now, Tyre?"

"What did you tell her?" Redburn's voice had taken on a note of deadliness.

"Not how fast you quit the high country," Starbright said. "And not how Walking Crow would ruin you for her, should he catch you. Man, you were crazy to try and lead a wagon company through here."

"I'm going to Oregon," Redburn answered. "I didn't ask for the job. They knew about my experience in the West and elected me to it. Moreover, I didn't think Walking Crow would nurse his grudge this long."

"Probably," said Starbright, "you didn't

hear what happened to The Pheasant after you ran out on her. They found her at the bottom of the Red Wall cliffs. She wasn't playing fast and loose the way you were. You knew the rules. There's two ways a white man does business with an Indian woman. He can offer a price and she can take it and everybody's satisfied. If there's no bargain and he still takes her, then he's taking her to wife. That's what they figure, and you knew it good and well. There wasn't any price with The Pheasant. It would have been insulting to offer it. Yet you enjoyed her to your fill, and she woke up to find she didn't have a husband."

"She had her fun, too, didn't she?" Redburn snapped.

"Not afterward, anyhow. No woman's having fun when she goes over a cliff. She was heart-broken, Redburn. The whole story was there for Walking Crow to read. He minded how you'd hung around her, him trusting you. He put it together."

"It could have been any white man in the high country," Redburn said.

"You know better than that."

"And I remember," said Redburn, "that you were pretty gone on her, yourself. So it's not me you're trying to protect from that greasy redskin chief."

"Only your people," Starbright agreed.

"Then I'll make you an offer. Personally,

I wouldn't mind twisting Walking Crow's nose again. But I agree with you about the company. I'll dodge you for its sake on one condition. You keep your mouth shut and see the other Fort Laramie men do, too."

"I'm not given to a loose tongue," Starbright retorted. "Neither are the other boys."

"I hope nobody proves to be that foolish," Redburn said. His voice carried a silky warning.

Starbright started back to the fort. He had succeeded in stopping the train, but it was yet to be proved that Walking Crow could be coaxed into leaving before the train came in. It couldn't camp long on the trail, and a Sioux knew how to be patient.

It was clear to Starbright that he and Redburn were out of two different worlds; Starbright had never understood the other man. Redburn had laughter, and yet a quick and deadly grimness. He had culture with still an animal's ferocity, which could spring instantly to action, and there were raw animal appetites behind his apparently fastidious tastes.

Tyre Redburn had shown up at Fort Laramie some four years past. He had been enough a part of the fur brigade to have won the puzzled respect of his fellow traders, one of them and yet apart from them, joining in as it suited him or isolating himself with total indifference. It was as if he had come here to purge himself of something intolerable and that accomplished had gone back to his civilization.

Now he had returned to the high country, though meaning only to pass through, with people who could know even less about him than did Dix Starbright.

CHAPTER THREE

The Indian camp had been made on the flat before Fort Laramie and it had an ominous quiet. Riding in to the fort, Starbright saw nothing to indicate that a feast was anticipated. When he had put up his horse, he went directly to the quarters of Lamont. He found the trader looking glum.

"I need your help again, Dix," said Lamont. "I got nowhere with Walking Crow. He wants no feast and he wants no gifts. He's just sitting here waiting for the wagons. He doesn't even say what he means to do. If it's a massacree, we couldn't stop it."

"I stopped Redburn until tomorrow," Starbright said. "That gives us a little time."

Lamont's face brightened. "I tell you what we should do then, Dix. For the sake of the settlers, we should take Redburn ourselves and turn him over to the Sioux. It wouldn't trouble me to see Redburn pay for his fun."

"Me, neither," Starbright agreed. "But Walking Crow don't want our help. Still, I used to have some influence with him. I'll go and see him."

"Would you, Dix?" said Lamont, relieved.

Striding toward the strangely quiet camp of

the Sioux, Starbright felt a nettling rebellion. The issue was not of his contriving, nor should its outcome be his responsibility. This situation had arisen from two deliberate acts of Redburn, one causing him to flee the high country, the other bringing him defiantly back. But for a nagging conscience, Starbright would have let Redburn see it through as he would. And except for the settlers. Starbright admitted a genuine concern, an instinctive sympathy for them. Rough people like himself, the emigrants were only seeking a decent chance to live as they chose. That had brought Dix Starbright to the Rockies, and that he had in common with them. He would respect that bond.

Starbright tramped directly to the largest lodge in the line. There he called the name of Walking Crow. A squaw responded, and then Starbright stood within, staring at the head of the village.

The Indian sat on a couch of buffalo robes, with a pillow of white deerskin and a frame of sprouts and reeds to support his back. His quiver and bow hung atop the rack, and the dishes from which he had eaten were still before him. His squaw, broad-faced and rump-sprung, showed a visible uneasiness at this visit.

For a moment Starbright merely looked into the chief's deep black eyes, trying to detect in them some trace of the chief's former friendliness.

"Long ago," said Starbright in the chief's tongue, "you would have made me your son. So I come to plead with you, Walking Crow. In the name of The Pheasant, whom I loved as you loved. In honor, and not as a thief."

The Indian was middle-aged, not tall but lending the impression of hard-fleshed weight. His coarse black hair, evenly parted, was divided into two braids that dropped over either side of his chest. He wore a metal bracelet on each wrist. His legs were stuffed into clean buckskin.

"Once," said Walking Crow, "is not now. I have no love left."

A wave of the man's hand, then, and Starbright seated himself upon another buffalo robe. A grunt to the squaw, and she started to prepare the pipe. At least Starbright was being received as a friend. Nothing more would be said until the pipe was smoked.

After that ceremony, Walking Crow crossed his thick legs and grasped an ankle with either hand. His eyes were beady probes on Starbright.

"Is it Redburn you want?" Starbright said then. "Or do you mean to have revenge against his whole people?"

"The man and his people are one," the

chief said. "As The Pheasant and her people were one."

Starbright shook his head. "The man's people want only to pass through this country and be gone. They did not help Redburn betray your village and your lodge. They know nothing about that, at all. I could not take the favor when you offered me The Pheasant for my wife. I loved her and wanted her, but it was not in my heart to stay in this country always. So it would not have been good for me to have her. That is what I told you then, and I stole nothing. Is that true, Walking Crow?"

"That is true," the chief said.

"Then," said Starbright, "I will take a favor now. The wagon people are my people, the same as they are Redburn's. If he and his people are one, his people and I are one. In hurting them, you would hurt me. Can you say that is not true?"

For a moment something streaked the chief's eyes. Unlike many white people who so often derided them, the Indians had a sense of friendship, of loyalty and honor that was not easily put aside. For an instant the Indian's stolid face showed expression, almost a pleading that Starbright not crowd his wish. Starbright stonily refused to yield.

"I cannot say it," said Walking Crow.

"Then let my people pass through your country without trouble."

"I will tell you," said Walking Crow, "what it is that I mean to do. My brother hunted with another village many sleeps down the river. He saw the white wagons and when they went in to feast he saw the man Redburn. They looked long into each other's eyes. He saw that there is a beautiful white woman there. My brother looked long at that woman, too. He will know her another time."

Starbright had lifted his shoulders. "The woman is not Redburn," he said sharply.

"Redburn cares for the woman. They were together. They laughed and touched hands."

"You mean to steal her? Is that why you are here?"

"I came only to tell Redburn what I will do before the white wagons have crossed the mountains. He will ride and sleep wondering when I will do to his woman what he did to my daughter."

"I will change the favor I asked," said Starbright. "Will you take your village away in the morning and let me tell Redburn what you mean to do to him?"

"You would try to trick me."

"I would."

Starbright watched his suggestion make its slow appeal to the chief. Walking Crow was himself wily. He respected that trait in others and liked a game of wits. He was bound to grant Starbright a favor, anyway, and this seemed to be acceptable to him. The chief nodded his head several times before he spoke.

"So be it. We will see if you can trick me."

When Starbright emerged from the fort the next morning the Sioux village had been dismantled and nothing remained but its litter. He was not deeply relieved at the change, which left him with the knowledge that the crisis had only been postponed. Danger would ride with the wagons from here to the pass, for weeks to come. The soul of Walking Crow could not know peace until he had done to Redburn as Redburn had done to him.

In the late afternoon the wagons appeared beyond the Laramie River, spilling out of the hills. They reached the stream, splashed aggressively across, and slowly came up the near climb. Thereafter they rolled straight to the fort, Redburn ahorse and visible to those who watched at the fort's gate. The lumbering vehicles drew slowly into their familiar circle. Starbright went to his room in the fort's deep interior. The newcomers had cost him enough bother, and he wanted a rest from them.

Thus it was that anger shot through him when, dozing in his room, racket in the central compound roused him. He knew immediately what it was, having experienced it before. The wagon people had invaded the fort to its innermost recesses, neither invited nor to be discouraged. Starbright had stripped to a breechcloth and moccasins for comfort in the heat. Sweat glistened on his brown upper body, his hair was tousled, and his face stubbled by a day's growth of beard.

He looked more ferocious than he realized when he stepped onto the gallery and glared down into the crowded yard.

"If you people must trespass," he bawled, "the least you could do is be quiet about it!"

It was as he had anticipated. The courtyard milled with curious settlers, the gawky, brassy and eternal American sightseer. But Starbright found himself staring down into the eyes of Rita Lang, who looked up in astonishment. For a moment he could only look at her, for she seemed apart from the press about her. Today she wore gingham that was fresh and neat. It was his first thorough look at her, and he openly indulged his interest.

She was as tall and dark and lithe as he had judged. Her frowning eyes were an agate brown and were staring at him angrily. She was clearly stung by his temper.

Rita said, "Where's your collar and chain?" Unabashed, she raked his all but naked body with the same point-by-point interest he had given hers. It was not boldness. She was showing him her awareness of his speculative study and her opinion of it.

"Too hot," said Starbright. "So I took it off. Ma'am, it happens this part of the fort's private. Trading post's in front. You people have no business back here. But you always come as if you owned it yourselves. That's a bad attitude. It's what's getting so many of you scalped and butchered."

"Is this fort your property?" Rita asked. "Are these your squaws and children?"

"There's a few strays mixed in," Starbright said promptly. "As to the fort, it's not yours and you've got no right back here."

Tyre Redburn shouldered his way through the crowd and walked toward Rita. He looked up at Starbright, frowning when he saw the latter's attire. It amused Starbright, who recalled how fastidious the man had been in such matters as dress, table manners, belching, and a mountain man's free way of relieving himself when and where necessary. Yet Redburn had had no code at all when it came to women, to humanity, to death, or to life itself.

He said, "Hello, Dix. I told these people to have a look back here. If it's all right with Lamont, I think you can stand it." He took Rita's arm as if anxious to hurry her off.

"I got something to tell you, Tyre," Starbright called. "Come and see me when

42

you get rid of her." He swung around and went back into his room. He dressed and emerged again, irritated and restless. The settlers were doing their trading with Lamont and his *engages.* Starbright drifted to the corral, half decided to get a horse and see if a ride might take the restlessness out of him. There he found Lafferty, the Irish trapper, smoking his pipe in the solitude of a shady corner.

"How come?" asked Starbright. "Figured you'd be shining up to some Missouri gal."

"Damme," said Lafferty. "I got a notion to go to Oregon with you. Like wild country, but I like my own kind of people, too. Man can have both out there."

"What's she look like?" asked Starbright.

Lafferty grinned. "All right. She's a dandy. I bet you she ain't even been kissed real good. Betcha she would be afore we got to the pass if I went along."

"Come ahead," said Starbright. "The pass is only a short piece compared to the whole trail. No telling how far you'd get by the time we reached the Willamette." Then he remembered a question he had meant to ask Lafferty and added, "You see that Missouri tough who tried to stick up the Lang wagons? Man with a broken neck?"

"See him when they buried him," Lafferty said.

"Sure beats me what he wanted and where he come from."

"Nothing to it," Lafferty retorted. "Settlers say Kelly Lang's got a fortune in gold in that big wagon of his. Going to open a bank in Oregon City. They got no cash money out there. Only way he could get it there was haul it in his wagon or ship it around the Horn. Figured he'd rather have it where he could keep his eye on it. So he's hauling it. But them others with him are guards."

"They sure got come up on easy," Starbright reflected. "And that don't show where them toughs came from."

"Followed the train," Lafferty said. "Lang still thinks he's got a big secret. But one like that's as hard to keep as a preacher's daughter going to have a young 'un. The whole train's onto it." The man's eyes were full on Starbright's when he added, "and Tyre Redburn knows it, too."

Starbright gave him a quick stare. "He's after the girl."

"What's wrong with a girl and gold both?"

Dismissing the impulse to take a ride, Starbright walked back to the fort, now turned moody and thoughtful. It had seemed odd to him that Redburn would let the Lang wagons fall back in Indian country without a heavier guard. Starbright shook his head but suspicions crawled into his mind. Gold in a quantity sufficient to enable Kelly Lang to start a bank would be an explosive factor in a train as large and conglomerate as the one out on the flat. Maybe Lang had trusted somebody it had been unwise to trust.

Lafferty was probably right about the three mysterious toughs having stalked the train all the way from the settlements, watching for a chance to jump the Lang outfit. Maybe they were acting on their own initiative, or again they could be working for somebody now in the train. Lafferty's suspicions had gone straight to the man who could have been the traitor.

Gnawing his pipestem at the fort gate, Starbright found his interest drawn to a man who stood out from the settler company. The fellow had taken notice of two Indian boys at play outside the walls, one of them limping on an obviously sore foot. The well-dressed emigrant had managed to overcome the fear of the half-savage child and was now trying to look at the foot. He was having no success.

Seeing Starbright's interest, the man called, "Do you speak this fellow's language, friend?" The voice was pleasant.

Starbright walked over. The man was young and physically frail, yet there was a look of strength in his face. He pointed to

45

the boy's foot, adding, "He's got a bad infection there. It ought to be treated."

The boy's great toe was swollen, Starbright observed, angry-looking and wholly unattended. "You a doctor?" Starbright asked the man.

"Doctor Wagner, sir. Medical missionary bound for the Lee Mission on the Willamette."

"That mean a preacher, too?" Starbright asked.

"I guess it does. You?"

"They call me Starbright. You want to operate on this boy's toe?"

"If he'll let me."

"Sooner have you scalp him," Starbright said. He spoke in dialect to the boy, saying, "The man is the white people's medicine man. He says he can make your foot well if you'll let him. Take him to your mother and ask what she thinks."

The boy moved off uncertainly. When Starbright had translated his remarks, the doctor followed. The incident left Starbright cheered, reminding him that there were motives other than self-interest in the wagon company.

When the supper hour arrived and passed without Redburn again presenting himself at the fort, Starbright struck out toward the encamped wagons. The smoke of a hundred cookfires lifted above the great circle. At a distance along the river grazed the big loose herd of livestock. The lowering sun struck pale fire to the wagon sheets and silhouetted the throng of people.

Starbright cut an angle to his right, seeking the figure of Tyre Redburn. He had passed half around the circle before he saw him. As a mountain man, Redburn had employed saddle and pack horses. Now he sported a wagon. There was another man in his camp, Starbright saw with a frown, making a talk here impossible.

Redburn gave him a close look, then said, "Hello, Dix. Looking for me?"

"Not from choice," Starbright said. "Thought I told you I had a message for you."

Frowning, Redburn said, "That's Cob Boze, Dix. He drives my wagon."

Starbright nodded but did not offer his hand to Boze. He knew the man's breed and didn't need to be told that Redburn had picked him up from the shacks of St. Louis or Independence, an opportunist looking for easy pickings.

"You mean he can hear what Walking Crow wanted me to tell you?" Starbright asked.

Redburn gave a start. "That one again? All right, let's take a walk."

Starbright moved behind the man while Redburn walked out into the sage. Presently Redburn halted and half turned, letting Starbright come up.

"What's new from Walking Crow, Dix?"

"Something he figured to tell you himself. I got him to leave by promising I'd do it for him. Man, you'd damned well better listen. He knows you've got your eye on a pretty girl again. In this train. I take it that would be Rita Lang."

Redburn straightened. "What about her?"

"Walking Crow means to pay you off in your own coin. He said he'll take her before you get out of this country. He means it, too."

"You're crazy!" Redburn breathed. But it was a protest and not a contradiction. Redburn believed what he had heard. He was frightened finally, with no wish to hide it. On a note of desperation, he added, "Then I've got to do something."

"You sure have," Starbright agreed. "You've got to quit this train. At least until it's crossed the divide."

"I couldn't. How would I explain it?"

"Rather risk the girl than run the risk of being found out, would you?"

"Why's either necessary?" Redburn asked harshly. "There's a way around it, Dix. Kelly Lang has been wanting to hunt buffalo. Rita, too. I haven't had a chance to take them out, myself. It wouldn't do for me to do so now. But Lafferty told me you're going to Oregon, yourself. You take the Langs hunting. You could give Walking Crow the slip with Rita and meet me and the wagons at Pacific Springs. Across the divide and past his country. Then he'd give it up."

"Not me," said Starbright.

"Doesn't it make sense?"

"Well — it does. But why should I?"

"You know what he'd do to her, Dix. Protecting her would bring the whole company into danger. You know that."

"Whisking her off wouldn't stop that."

Redburn made a helpless, pleading motion with his hands. "Neither would keeping her with the train."

"Then you both leave the train," Starbright retorted, "and I'll get word to Walking Crow you've done so. That protects the train, and that's what's important. The hell with you and Rita Lang," he snapped, turning to leave.

"Wait, damn you! I'd take the Langs hunting and ask you to take the train to Pacific Springs. But I don't know the country we'd have to go through. I never visited it in the old days. You know the country. Moreover, you're better at dodging Indians than I am. Dix, you've got to do it for Rita's sake. If you will, I'll make you a promise. If there's so much as the threat of an attack on the train, meanwhile, I'll give myself up to Walking Crow."

"I couldn't depend on that," said Starbright; then he paused to consider. If

Lafferty joined the wagon company, he certainly could be depended upon to see that Redburn kept the promise. He had little doubt that Lafferty would do it, for there were a pair of lips to draw him. "All right," he amended. "I'll do it. What did you have in mind for a hunting trip?"

Relief flooded Redburn's face. "We'll probably have no trouble from Walking Crow until we come to the Sweetwater and close to his own country. You could travel with the train that far and help me keep an eye on Rita. Someplace short of the Sweetwater, you could slip away in a manner to give Walking Crow's spies the slip. Then cross the Laramies and hunt south of the Greens and the Trail. You'd save distance and travel faster and gain time to hunt."

"It might work," Starbright admitted. "When are you trailing again?"

"Day after tomorrow. Now, come and talk it over with the Langs. They'll be delighted." Redburn seemed wholly relieved and was his gay self again. He struck off toward the wagon linen.

Still doubtful but feeling he had made the best of a bad situation, Starbright followed. The elaborate camp of the Langs was on the river side of the circle. Starbright had seen the big wagon, and he needed but one glance at the camp to understand why Redburn was so jumpy about his reputation with the Langs.

The massive wagon was the type jeeringly called a palace car, especially built for comfort. Kelly Lang sat in a portable easy chair, shaded by the fly of the tent and smoking a calabash pipe. Now he wore boots and well-pressed trousers, and had topped that off with an ornate buckskin shirt. His face, clean-shaved except for mustache, showed a prairie tan. It was a strong face, Starbright thought, and the eyes were level and fearless.

"Maybe," Redburn said to the man, "you can have your hunt after all, Mr. Lang. I guess you've already met Dix Starbright. There isn't a better guide in the mountains. I found out that he's heading for Oregon, himself. So I talked him into helping you hunt south of the trail from here to the pass."

Kelly Lang rose. "Why, fine." He offered Starbright his hand. There was strength in his grip, and a cool assurance in his manner. "He won't be sorry."

"Don't offer him pay," Redburn warned. "A mountain man's got a touchy pride. Dix is doing it as a favor to me."

"How many will there be?" Starbright asked.

"My daughter and I," Lang answered. "Probably a couple of others. When do we start?"

"When I figure it's time," Starbright said curtly.

Redburn laughed uneasily. "He eats bearmeat raw, Mr. Lang. But he'll find you game, dodge the Indians, and get you to Pacific Springs safely." Then he nodded and left.

Lang said, "We were all pretty rattled the other night. I don't remember that I thanked you, Starbright."

"Someplace you played the fool, mister, in letting it get out that you're hauling gold."

Kelly Lang's shoulders pulled up and he gave Starbright a quick, hard stare. "Where did you hear that?"

Starbright grinned. "From a trapper at the fort."

"I'll be damned!" Lang breathed.

"Wondering who leaked it?" Starbright asked.

"Wondering a lot of things," Lang said musingly. Then, giving the buckskin man a close look, he added, "How would you like to join my outfit permanently? All the way to the settlements, as well as for the hunting trip."

"Not me," said Starbright. "Once we get to the pass, I aim to dust it. Your wagons are far too slow. But I'll give you some advice. Whoever you trusted with your secret is a good man for you to watch out for."

"I trusted no one," Lang retorted. "I have a partner in this venture. He's the only one who knows anything about my business."

"Then watch *him*," said Starbright.

"He's leading this company," Lang said.

Sucking in a noisy breath, Starbright said, "Redburn your partner?"

"What's so strange about that? He knows the frontier, and I don't. In fact, he interested me in the Oregon settlements."

"What's he putting up?" Starbright asked bluntly.

"It's a fifty-fifty arrangement. Dollar for dollar, if you please."

That astonished Starbright. He knew that Redburn could not have made money of the kind Lang would have in mind, either in the fur trade or since he had left it. But the man might have come from a wealthy family. Starbright decided that he had already said too much.

Rita Lang came along the wagon line, returning to her camp. She gave a start when she saw Starbright, then came on with a cool lift of the head. She seemed surprised when her father told her of the proposed hunting trip, but not displeased.

"That's kind of you," she told Starbright. "And I'm surprised you'd do it."

"He's going to Oregon to live," Kelly Lang put in.

"He is? With our train?"

"Only as far as the pass," Starbright reiterated. "And seeing that we'll be saddle-

mates that far, we better have an understanding. It'll be a tough trail I'll take you
over. I won't spare you a whit."

"Think I'm soft?"

"I'll find out." Starbright touched his cap
and took his leave.

CHAPTER FOUR

Starbright slept at the fort the last night. He was at the wagon camp with saddle and pack horses when dawn broke over the big flat. It was a well-organized train, he found; Redburn seemed to know his business. Men rode out to round up the loose stock, and the teams to go under draft that day were brought in to the wagons. Cookfires sent a hundred separate smokes into the clean, cool air. A breeze rippled the sage, moving on toward the mountains.

The emigrants were grave, swift-moving, keyed up for the resumed march. They had rested and reprovisioned, and in their busy industry were quietly cheerful. Starbright kept apart with his animals, having decided with Redburn that he could be more useful if he outrode the train and kept his eyes open for trouble.

Lafferty was coming along but he had thrown in with a wagon party, a settler with two pretty daughters, one of which was causing a big change in Lafferty's life.

One by one breakfasts were finished and camps broken. Watching idly, Starbright again revised his opinion of the settlers. Rough and impoverished as most of them were, they had a sober steadfastness, an iron discipline and diligence. The greater part of the wagons and livestock showed attention and was in the best of shape, considering the punishment of the long trail. Nowhere did Starbright see a duplication of Kelly Lang's sumptuous outfit. The others had good wagons, a few only two-wheeled carts, together with the stock to pull it and a minimum of furnishings and equipment for a new start on the far western frontier.

The trail out of Laramie ran west, crossing flats closehugged by crinkled hills and sheer bluffs. The hours slipped by, and Starbright's watch of the surroundings disclosed nothing worrisome. Midmorning found the country growing rougher. Starbright kept ahead and alone during the noon halt. The sun at its zenith stood baldly above him but its heat was tempered by the hill country's gentle drafts.

Starbright stopped at the warm springs with considerable daylight remaining that he would have preferred to use in travel. The spring was not hot but gave forth water sufficiently warm to be attractive for bathing and laundering. The train would halt here for the night, so Starbright moved forward a half mile before picking a place for his own camp.

When he had dropped pack he led his

horses to the river to drink and cool their hoofs. Returned to his camp, he cooked his supper, taking a mixed attitude in his detachment from the people he had not brought himself to embrace. Yet the proximity of so many people gave this camp a loneliness he had never felt on the old fur trails.

When dusk rolled in he found that his privacy was not going to be respected. The picketed horses swung their heads to look toward the main camp. Close listening brought to Starbright no awareness of an on-coming animal. Watching the near-by skyline, he soon saw two shapes outlined against the fading light; the figures of a man and woman on foot.

Starbright stood up, took the pipe from his mouth, and was still staring when they came up to his fire. They came close before he recognized Wagner, the man who had called himself a medical missionary.

Starbright could not remember having seen the girl who accompanied Wagner. He knew that he would have been impressed for she was striking. The firelight falling upon her disclosed a wealth of blonde hair. Her nose was small, her eyes wide apart, her mouth wearing a friendly smile for Starbright. She was small in build and plainly dressed, yet Starbright felt a full stir of male interest as he studied her.

"Good evening, Starbright," Wagner said pleasantly. "I'd like to present you to Liz Templeton. Miss as yet. Missus, perhaps, when we can find another preacher. Walking all day isn't enough for her. She has to stretch her legs again before bedtime."

"He's lying all around," said Liz, offering Starbright a small brown hand. "Except for the miss, which I intend to remain until I've looked over the field out here. As for the leg-stretching, I was simply curious to see you — as part of the field. So I made Ralph bring me out."

"This is no country," Starbright said sharply, "for the likes of you to poke around in after dark by yourselves."

"He's got a point," said Wagner. "And that's the second time tonight you've been told that."

"If that's coffee on the fire," Liz retorted, "I'd like a cup. Don't scowl at me, Ralph."

Wagner, Starbright observed, was not really frowning at the pert girl. Though reproving, he was amused by her mood. There was more than that involved, though, the mountain man suspected. The medical missionary was more than fond of Liz Templeton.

"Sit down," Starbright invited. He had only one cup, which he filled with coffee from the battered black pot on the fire. Without spilling a drop, Liz, holding the cup, seated herself in lithe Indian fashion by his blaze.

She sipped the coffee, letting her eyes appraise Starbright with frank interest.

To his surprise, Starbright saw Ralph Wagner pull out a pipe. The man apparently was far less stiff-necked than the preachers Starbright had known as a boy. Starbright reached for his own pipe, a sense of contentment rising in him.

"I hear you're taking a hunting party out," Wagner said. "Liz wants to go along."

"No chance," said Starbright.

"Thank Heaven," Liz breathed. "I didn't want to go, but my hoyden reputation compelled me to act like I did. Tell me something, Dix Starbright. You scolded us for coming out here alone. Yet you travel by yourself. What's the difference?"

"Six years in this country. That makes a whale of a difference."

They left presently, and Starbright found himself reluctant to see them go. He saw their hands reach out and clasp as they went over the top-of-land. Now Dix Starbright felt deeply lonely at his solitary fire. . . .

Once more Starbright sat his horse in the dawn and watched the emigrant camp break up. It was a well-defined movement with which he was growing familiar, herders moving out through the loose stock, which had scattered in the night, and starting it in toward the camp, each man examining a sector of the outer arc for signs of strays to

59

be hunted. Thereafter came the milling of animals and people, the quick striking of tents, the reloading of overnight supplies — then the wagons were back on the trail.

They moved past Starbright's point of vantage, in parallel and spaced-out strings. The space between the lines held the loose animals in herd and guided them, the whole contingent dissolving and reappearing in the great, rolling cloud of dust. Except for the old and infirm and the women with young children, this was a walking company, setting forth at sunrise and trudging patiently through the long day, following the sun toward the place where it would set.

That night Starbright found a place for himself in the wagon circle. He found himself only a few wagons away from those of the Lang party. He cooked his supper in the gathering dusk, for the first time in years finding comfort in having great numbers of people about him. He was going to the settlements, where these settlers or ones like them would become his neighbors. It was time he learned how to mix with his own kind again.

Yet they left him alone, and he realized that he already had built himself a stand-offish reputation. Lafferty looked him up for a few words but was soon off to get back to his new friends. Then from somewhere music struck up in the night, a fiddle, an accordion, and a guitar. People began to move past Starbright's camp, gay and noisy, seeking the music's source.

Presently he could tell by the distant racket and movement that a prairie dance was in progress under the stars. He didn't move down there, although he saw Kelly Lang and some of the men in his party go past. Starbright wondered why Rita had not wanted to dance, why Redburn had not come for her.

Then, to his surprise, she came walking up to his camp, idly strolling.

"Who's watching the gold?" Starbright greeted her.

The firelight fell on her face, showing him that she was in good humor. She smiled and said, "Since its presence has been so widely advertised, it ought also to be published that it wouldn't be easy to steal. It's in an iron chest, and the chest is bolted to the wagon bed."

"Whole wagon could be stolen," said Starbright.

Rita was appraising him, although she shook her head when he motioned her to be seated. Again he tried to measure her in return. She was fiery, restless and wilful, certainly, and he knew already that she was given to extremes of mood. Her mouth and eyes hinted at a passion that he suspected could rule her. She had a taste for the game of promise and withdrawal, there was no mistaking that.

She said, "Well, shall we trade insults again? What are you finding in me, Starbright?"

"Woman without too much sense. What do you see?"

"A brute. Handsome, sure enough, but savage to the core."

"That's a fact," said Starbright. "Don't let yourself be come upon alone by me. I know what I want and I take what I want where I find it. You're safe only if I'm right in my feeling that you ain't got it."

Her head came back. She was half amused and half irritated again. She started to speak, hesitated, then moved on, angling out from the wagons to be quickly swallowed in the sage.

Starbright felt his heart hit his ribs and begin to hammer. He rose and followed her, his moccasins making no sound. Cutting into the sage, he moved around her, meaning to get ahead and present himself to her. She had been a little too taunting, a little too sure of herself and his obedience of the rules she relied upon to protect her. Moreover, it was no country for her to poke around in alone, and she needed to be shown that even more than did the overconfident Liz Templeton. Rita didn't know than an Indian chief wanted her badly.

Starbright knew when he passed her that she was expecting him to follow her for she glanced back. He slipped on ahead of her to a point she would have to pass. There he lost sight of her and waited, grinning.

He was there a long while before deciding that she had turned back to camp. Then a mocking voice nearby said, "What are you doing over there, Starbright? Waiting for somebody?" He heard Rita's throaty laugh, then the sound of her running back toward the wagon camp.

His cheeks stung and he felt like a fool. He had walked right into her trap. She had teased, then outguessed and outprowled him. She had had her taste of triumph over him. But Starbright grinned again as he started back. She would pay for that little caper. He didn't try to catch her. His chance would come.

For two untroubled days the wagons moved up the Platte. The country grew rougher, rock cropping out more frequently, and once there was a descent so abrupt that the wagons had to be roped down. Starbright stayed with the train now because of the growing problems of the trail itself. He found that he was not badly needed. Redburn kept the wagons moving steadily onward and, on the second night after Warm Spring they found themselves at the river crossing.

It also had brought them close to the

country Walking Crow regarded as his own. Seeking Redburn, Starbright said, "How long will it take you to get to the divide?"

"We'll crowd it," said Redburn. "I'm not anxious for you to have my girl away from me a day longer than necessary. You be at Pacific Springs in two weeks. I'll try to make it. If I don't, it's a good place for you to camp. Now, you'd better tell me just what you plan on."

"I'll follow the La Bonte into the hills," Starbright said. "Then cross over to the basin."

Redburn looked surprised. "That's mean country."

"But it don't draw Sioux."

"That's right. What then?"

"We'll go between the Greens and Sweetwater to the divide. Tell Lang we'll pull out around midnight. Two horses each and no more. I don't want any cavalry troop. Their guns, bedding, and two weeks' rations. No damned fool dodads."

Redburn grinned. "I don't blame you there. Kelly Lang likes to do his roughing-it in comfort. I'll tell him. And get this, Starbright. To my mind, what's done is done. We'll get out of Walking Crow's runways as soon as possible. Afterward I want to forget it and I wish you would, too."

"I wouldn't be going to this trouble," Starbright retorted, "if I had the stomach to tell your girl the kind of record you chalked up out here. I got something to tell you, too, man, and I'll do more than hint. Sacrifice somebody other than yourself to pay your bill with the Sioux, and I'll kill you."

"If it comes to a showdown," Redburn said angrily, "I'll do what I promised. I'll face that devil alone and have it out with him."

"I'll be waiting at the springs," Starbright said. "And I'll be right curious on that score. Now, go tell your friends to get ready."

Starbright himself had little to do to prepare for the hunting expedition though he had a private step to take. He found Lafferty and told him what so far had been a secret between himself and Redburn. "I don't trust Redburn to play the hero," he concluded, "if it comes to saving his train. Lafferty, if you smell trouble and there's no other way, you take Redburn to Walking Crow, yourself."

"Just give me a chance," Lafferty replied.

Around ten o'clock, with the main company bedded down, Starbright went over to the Lang camp to check with them. He found Rita and her father with two others who were members of the Lang party. He was introduced to the pair, Elvek and Gardiner. They were busy making up packs, and

Starbright noted the array of shooting irons, the copious ammunition. But Redburn had relayed Starbright's instructions. The packs were right. The orders had been obeyed to the letter.

It was the first time Starbright had seen Rita close since the incident in the sage-brush. She smiled at him sweetly and at the first chance said, "It's so nice of you to take us out, Starbright. It's to be hoped that you're better at stalking game than defense-less women."

"Defenseless!" Starbright snorted.

In her triumph her eyes were warm and friendly. She was dressed for riding, wearing a habit of plain and durable material, together with heavy boots.

He added, "I'm glad you're starting out cocky. We'll see how long it takes to wear that off."

"You still think I'm too soft to ride your trails, do you?"

"Soon know, anyhow," said Starbright.

CHAPTER FIVE

The hunting party was ready to start before midnight. Starbright led the way, the pack animals strung out, Lang and Rita flanking the string, and the two others bringing up the rear. They headed due west, following the south bank of the river. They pressed on until the heat of the next day before making camp. By then they had entered the lower rises of the Laramies with their scattered, parklike stands of forest, and were at the headwaters of the La Bonte.

His charges showed punishment but not one complained. Starbright felt worn himself for all of them had trailed a day with the wagons before making this long ride. But his mind had eased. The chances were good that they had slipped away without warning the spies Walking Crow would undoubtedly have left to watch the wagon company.

Camped in the trees beside the creek, they fixed a meal. While they ate it, Starbright outlined their itinerary, concluding, "We've got less distance to travel than the wagons. Horseback's twice as fast. That's how we'll gain a week to hunt in. Now, get some sleep."

He didn't go to bed immediately himself. Going down to the sandy bank of the creek, he cut willow sprouts and hunted up a likely pool below a riffle. Presently he had built a small fish trap with braided sprouts that formed a pen with a narrow opening. Trout would wander into the pen and a great many of them would be unable to find their way out again.

Starbright was up at dawn, and by the time he had started a fire the others had stirred forth. Sleepy-eyed, Rita said, "What's for breakfast, Starbright?"

"Come on," Starbright said, "and I'll show you."

The fish trap was full. The girl stared into the limpid water in surprise. "Hundreds of them! We can't eat them all!"

"We can try," said Starbright. "Know how to clean a fish?"

"Certainly."

"Fine." Starbright gave her his knife. "Clean a couple dozen. The biggest ones."

"What do you know!" breathed Rita. "He knows how to work nature for all it's worth. You at least know how to trap a trout, Starbright." The brown eyes laughed at him.

She cleaned the fish, too. Then she elbowed him away from the fire and cooked the trout herself. Rolled in cornmeal and fried, they came out better than Starbright could have prepared them.

Afterward the party started off on a hunt. They had gone but a short distance when they saw three deer coming out of the forward hills, moving down to the water. Starbright signaled a halt. They left their horses in the hollow and moved forward to the top of the ridge.

"Drop flat," Starbright whispered. "When I signal, bang away."

It was a long moment before the deer came up out of the draw. They were farther over than Starbright had hoped for, making all but impossible targets for the greenhorns. But nobody got buck fever. The silence held. Then four guns cracked at his signal.

Starbright blinked when one of the deer fell in its tracks, the buck, while the others bounded off through the sage. His eyes narrowed again when a second staggered and went down on the slope of the ridge. The third toppled only a half length short of the ridge top.

"Now, who wasted a bullet?" he asked sourly.

Rita was up and running forward. Starbright followed, the others ambling behind. The girl took a look at the first carcass and was smiling broadly as the men came up. Starbright's mouth dropped open. Two slugs had torn through the buck's brain.

"Whom do I share the honors with?" Rita asked.

Her father was eying Starbright in amusement. "Your proud sire. Starbright, have you ever scouted the country east of the Mississippi? You'd ought to. There's a little big game back there, too."

Starbright said to Rita, "Know how to dress a deer?"

"Now, look, Starbright!"

"Since my shot probably landed first," Lang said expansively, "I'll take care of that. Rita will get her work cooking. Starbright, wait till you've tasted her roasted ribs."

"The deer's ribs, that is," said Rita, and her eyes made wicked lights at Starbright.

They broke camp early the next morning, packing the ponies and striking out into the higher hills. Twice during the morning they scared up more deer, but Starbright refused to allow further shooting. The way grew more difficult, but around noon they crossed the sharp ridge of the Laramies, not long afterward emerging into a vast and seemingly lifeless basin.

Starbright made a sweeping gesture with his arm, saying, "We'll have a lot of that stuff from here to the upper Platte."

At this viewpoint the country ahead was a forbidding sight. The sun hung nakedly in the forward distance. Its heat and glare

70

seemed to have cooked the vitality out of the stunted sage and twisted greasewood of the bottom. It burned upon the eroded bluffs and sharpened their awesome contours.

Clinging to the foothills, they reached the headwaters of another creek for their next camp. Starbright was not disturbed by the discontent he now saw plainly in his party. Even had it been wise, he would not have told them that they were here for a reason starkly different to what they supposed. So Starbright stuck to his real purpose, protecting Rita, and let them harbor their resentments and growing restiveness.

The party was willing to press on the next day rather than to lay over as Starbright offered. They kept skirting the basin, Starbright planning the route so as to find water for the night camp.

Again Lang and his people wanted to keep going. Pointing due west through another long, hot march, they came in late afternoon to the upper North Platte and the promise of a more inviting country. They had by then swung west of the regular haunts of Walking Crow. Starbright's charges had shown stamina and a lack of open complaint that surprised the mountain man considerably. He had sought to expose their weaknesses and had failed, and yet the defeat did not displease him.

He said, "From here on, we'll find better going."

Not long afterward they came to a well-worn Indian trail. A day's ride north, after that, would have put them back on the Overland, and Starbright found himself relieved by that knowledge. Then, an hour later, he pulled down his horse to lend a deep study to the forward country.

"What's the trouble?" asked Lang, riding up.

"A bird belched a mile off," said Rita. "It alarmed him."

"Thought I saw dust," Starbright said, frowning.

"Indians?" Lang asked.

"If so, it'd be a small party. But likely it was a go-devil. That's a pint-size whirlwind."

Low, bare butteland stretched before them, burning beneath the coppery sun. It had to be penetrated. Starbright made his decision and went on, the others falling into place behind. It was late afternoon, and Johnny Monohan's camp was too far distant to be reached that day.

The forward dust cleared out of the atmosphere, gone completely, yet Starbright found himself unable to ease up. When they dropped into a depression that shortened their vision, he said, "I'm going to take a look. You people keep on the way you're going, but take it easy."

"You're worried, aren't you?" Lang asked, his voice steady.

"Got a feeling," Starbright admitted.

Starbright rode off to the north, a plan quickly forming. When he had put himself half a mile above the trail, he turned west again, followed a ravine that kept him hidden. His eyes steadily searched the earth passing under his horse and the trail ahead.

Then, just short of the first hills, he came upon what he hunted and feared — fresh horse tracks, pointing south, and three different sets. They were shot horses, which was strong evidence that the riders were not Indians. Starbright flung one thoughtful glance north toward the Overland Trail, then looked south again. A spur of hills ran out a short distance from him. These riders had gone up into the hills. There was the chance that their destination was the Indian trail which they had been seeking to cut. They had ridden hard enough to raise dust.

Starbright turned along the line of the horse tracks. He pulled up a pistol. On the first rise, his own horse gave him warning.

Starbright prevented its nickering, then slid from the saddle. He led the horse by the cheek strap until he came upon other horses in a draw. Two of them wore riding saddles while the other was packed with camp equipment. Starbright knew then that the two riders were lying in wait on the Indian trail for the hunting party to appear. He realized also that he had no time to waste, for Lang and his people would ride into the trap without warning. Starbright left his horse with the others and prowled forward on foot.

The ravine crested, then broadened as it fell away. The men he followed wore boots, and presently the tracks left the bottom to move up the side of the hill. Starbright left them, picking a route of his own to the left. As he came over the brow of the hill, he saw the Lang party jogging on, less than a quarter mile away.

Forted up in the rocks below Starbright were the two strangers he stalked, each with a rifle and each with his attention riveted to the oncoming horses.

Holding a pistol in either hand, Starbright boomed, "Let go the rifles, boys! Stand up!"

He wanted a prisoner to question, but the next seconds showed him he had a fight, instead. He accepted it, for the shooting would warn Kelly Lang. Without moving otherwise, a man flung an arm across his body, his rifle swinging it. He shot in a burst of frantic action, stunned fear trapped on his face. Starbright chopped down, fired, and saw the ball kick into flesh.

The other man, cooler, slithered into the protection of the rocks. Starbright sailed down the slope. He saw the glint of a rifle barrel beside a rock; he saw a man desperately seeking a swift, sure shot. The rifle belched flame. Starbright's cap seemed to twist on his head but he felt nothing. Using the second pistol, he shot at the head and shoulders he could detect. He never missed a stride and was down upon the man before he realized this one was out of the fight. He had got both men through the head.

The Lang party had stopped its horses, still out of rifle range. Leaping onto a rock, Starbright waved arms and guns above his head. He saw them start on uncertainly. Then he took a better look at the trail wolves he had shot. They were homespun men. Their faces were like those of Cob Boze, the driver of Redburn's wagon, or of the first road runner encountered back beyond Fort Laramie.

Starbright had a sick feeling, partly in reaction to the sudden lethal violence and partly from something else. The only one he had outlined his itinerary to was Tyre Redburn. He hadn't even disclosed it to Lafferty. Yet these two Missouri wolves had known where to intercept him. *Me or Kelly Lang?* Starbright thought suddenly.

Then the others were on the scene, staring in horror at what they saw.

"Know 'em?" Starbright asked Lang.

The banker shook his head. "No, but they

could have been the two who got away the other time. When they tried for my wagon."

"They are," Starbright said.

"Ah," Lang breathed. "They thought this trip was an effort to slip the gold through safely."

"I reckon." But Starbright didn't believe that. His mind was red hot with suspicions that he was not prepared to divulge. "You trust the men you left with your wagon?"

"They've worked for me for years."

"Gold can change men fast, mister."

"I've had reasons to think that, myself," Lang admitted. "Think we should rejoin the train?"

Starbright had been considering that. But it wouldn't do. While the horseback party had pulled safely beyond the country frequented by Walking Crow, the wagons would as yet be in the middle of it and would be stalked by the chief at least as far as South Pass.

He said, "Likely there's no need. This is the end of that one gang, any how. We'll search them and their packs and see what we can learn about them."

The search that followed proved futile. There was nothing to disclose who the men were, where they came from, or if they had any particular connection with the wagon company they had tracked.

Another half day's travel brought them to

Johnny Monohan's trapper camp. At first glimpse it appeared to be a small Indian village set in a thin stand of pine above a little valley. There were half a dozen lodges but in their center stood a dog-trot cabin that belonged to the squaw man.

"The Injuns are Shoshone," Starbright said. "They're middling peaceful. These are shirt-tail relatives of Johnny's wives."

"Wives?" Rita asked.

"Johnny's only got a couple now," Starbright told her. "Ain't the man he used to be."

The dogs that cut loose as the horsemen drew nearer were also typical of an Indian encampment. Nobody tried to silence them.

Curious urchins showed solemn faces from every point of vantage. Starbright rode into the camp and saw Monohan standing in the doorway of the cabin, a giant of a man with wild gray whiskers and hair.

"Howdy, Johnny!" called Starbright. "I got some easterners who want to shoot their guns. Figured we might as well get some good of it if there's buffs about."

Johnny's eyes had kindled, and a grin had leaped to his rugged face. "Cuss me if it ain't Dix Starbright!" he roared and grasped Starbright's hand.

For the sake of quiet, Starbright chose a campsite a quarter mile up the river from the trapper camp.

Most of the men turned in early that night to rest for the next day's hunt. But, somehow restless and yet elated, Rita remained at the fire. Starbright found himself lingering to smoke an extra pipe.

"Tell me," said Rita, smiling at him, "did you ever have it like Johnny has?"

"How do you mean?" he asked gruffly.

"Squaws."

"How do you want me to answer that — that I had 'em or didn't?"

"Why would I care?"

"And," Starbright continued, "is it me you're curious about or Tyre Redburn when he was out before?"

That made Rita give a start. "Why did you think of him?"

"He's on your trail, and you're not running too hard to get away."

"I like Tyre. Probably I'll marry him. I wouldn't care if either of you'd had your moments with the Indian girls. It's tying up the way Johnny has and with numbers of them and breeding children by the dozens — that's sordid."

"You'd be surprised," said Starbright. "I've seen white marriages less happy."

"You call them marriages?" Rita gasped.

"What do you?"

"Cheap adulteries."

Starbright scowled. "Look here. They're marriages while they last. When they quit being marriages, they break up. They don't go on for years and years with the two people hating each other but swallowing it for the sake of respectability."

Rita laughed, then presently said, "What's between you and Tyre that's so deadly? The night you stopped the train from coming into Fort Laramie I heard enough to guess you're holding a threat over his head. That's what I'm driving at, tonight. Was it his fling with the squaws?"

"You'd have to ask him. And now I'm going to bed."

"Wait. I've been wanting to eat a little crow. We owe you a lot for breaking up that ambush before we rode into it. Much as it galls me to say it, you're as good as you seem to think you are."

"I'll do," said Starbright, "for a savage." He strode off into the darkness.

She was getting into him too deeply for his own good, he realized. She was too confident of herself and her mastery of the game she liked to play with him. She had a lesson coming, and Starbright still remembered that night in the sagebrush when she had called so tauntingly, "What are you doing over there, Starbright? Waiting for somebody?"

CHAPTER SIX

They killed two buffalo the next day, strays left by a passing herd. Starbright let them lay, intending to give most of the meat to Johnny Monohan in return for his squaws' butchering the great animals.

When Starbright returned from telling Johnny Monohan to put his relatives to work, he brought back an invitation to a feast for that evening.

"Eat with them?" Rita gasped. "What would we have?"

"A lot of queer things," Starbright informed her. "Including a good fat dog."

"I won't go."

"Better go. Even Johnny wouldn't like it if you didn't."

"I'll be sick," she said.

"Likely, but it won't kill you."

"Sick beforehand. That's a good civilized excuse, and I'll use it."

"Suit yourself," Starbright told her.

He thought she would change her mind, but as the day dwindled and it became time to go she was still stubborn. Starbright scowled at her. It wouldn't do to leave her alone in the camp, nor could he himself very well stay away from Johnny's feast. Yet he knew the rules of etiquette. If she attended the feast at all, she would be required to eat of every dish offered. Some would be certain to turn her stomach.

"You boys go on," Starbright said to the men. "You're the ones Johnny wants to put on the dog for. I'll try to fix it up with him tomorrow about me and Rita. She's civilized sick and she's given me a mean headache."

"Go on and eat your dog!" Rita blazed at him.

Kelly Lang left with the other two men. None of them looked eager, but they realized the propriety of their accepting the invitation. Rita had turned defiant. She busied herself with her pack as night closed in, acting as if Starbright were nowhere in the country.

At last Starbright rose and walked off into the timber. He went but a short distance, then sat down beneath a low-hanging pine and pulled out his pipe and tobacco. A warm mountain breeze fluted the pine needles, carrying to his sensitive nostrils the mysterious scents of the forest floor. Through a break in the treetops he could see the sky and a banner of blazing stars. Then at long last his ears caught the sound that he wanted to hear.

Rita came slowly through the trees, moving

with uncertainty. He knew that nervousness or loneliness might have stirred her forth. Yet, it could have been something else. He noticed suddenly that he was holding his breath. His heart made thunder in his ears, a wild well-being flushed through him.

He let her get almost past him before he spoke from his shelter.

"Not that way. Over here."

She whirled, giving out a quick, short cry. "I couldn't imagine what had happened to you!" she said. "Then I got to hearing all kinds of weird sounds."

"Why didn't you holler?"

He rose as she started to turn back. He put a hand on her shoulder when he overtook her, pulling her around. She flung a sobered upward look at him. He swept her from her feet, catching her lightly in his arms. She struggled, starting to cry out until he crushed his mouth to hers. So holding her, he walked back in under the pine boughs.

He placed her gently on the ground, and when she tried to rise he drew her tightly to him. She arched herself, trying to roll free, half gasping but not crying out. She kicked with her knees. She made a slashing sweep with her nails and he felt blood on his face.

She moaned, "Please — please — !" Then her body went limp and still.

But she tried to dodge his mouth. The

starlight showed him that her eyes were open, frightened and yet fearless. He began to whisper to her tenderly, saying only her name, "Rita . . . Rita . . . Rita . . ." He whispered the anger out of her eyes. He put a wonder there. She seemed not to notice the change when his lips grew quiet. He lay for a long moment of stillness, feeling her breathing in the breasts pressed to him and the wild race her heart gave his own. Her eyes were closed now and her mouth did not evade when he sought it again. At last her lips gave the kiss back to him.

Starbright pushed himself up quietly, gently. No muscle stirred in her slender, supine body. Her eyes were still closed as if the incompleteness held her in deep arrest.

"What you doing down there?" he whispered hoarsely. "Waiting for somebody?"

Turning, he started back to camp.

It was a long while before Rita came in. Yet she moved in full stride and was smiling slightly. She looked at Starbright for a long moment, and he could see that she had carefully brushed the pine needles from her skirt and blouse and smoothed her hair.

"What are you going to do about that scratch on your cheek, Starbright?" she murmured. She got her blankets and moved into the outer darkness again.

Starbright was smoking his pipe by a bed of coals when he heard the men returning from the feast. Their laughter and relaxed voices were almost a shock. The fires that had run in his flesh for the past two hours had all but exhausted him. Two regrets worried him, one that he had sought revenge at all, the other that he had taken it in preference to what he might have had.

Kelly Lang called, "Maybe it's a good thing Rita didn't come, Starbright. They had the dog. I had to excuse myself quietly and get sick behind Johnny's cabin."

"Lots of men do the first time," Starbright said. He turned his face fully to Lang. He had washed away the blood, and whiskers covered part of the scratch. Still there was a red, skinless streak under his left eye and over his exposed cheekbone. But the men scarcely looked at him as they prepared their beds.

It was not until breakfast time the next morning that Lang gave him a quick, hard stare and said, "What happened to your face?"

"Run into a limb last night," Starbright answered. He waited for Rita to light the fuse that would blow this hunting party apart.

But Rita smiled and said, "You should have heard him howl. It woke me up. Tell me, Dad, should I get Johnny's recipe for dog?"

"Never mind," said Lang, grinning.

Rita flashed her smile to Starbright, whose eyes conveyed his thanks. Yet her own told him that she was not yet done with their game.

For three days thereafter Starbright and his party hunted out of Monohan's camp. They had fair success. Then Starbright called a halt. Nine days had elapsed since they had left the wagons at the Platte crossing. The train by now should be somewhere along the Sweetwater, plodding toward South Pass in the Wind River range.

On the last evening, Starbright said to his party, "It'll take us three days pushing to get to what they call Pacific Springs. That's beyond the divide. I told Redburn we'd be there waiting. The wagons will need luck to get there as soon as he figured. But if they did, and we hadn't showed, they'd be worried."

"I guess we'd better go," Lang said with regret.

For three days thereafter Starbright traveled westward, leading the party. They paralleled the Overland Trail for much of that distance but never came closer to it than a dozen miles until they reached South Pass. There they picked up the Overland Trail. The last evening of travel brought them safely to Pacific Springs. There was evidence of earlier migration this season, but Starbright experienced a quick sense of satisfaction in the fact that the Redburn party had not yet arrived.

"You're in the Far West now," Starbright told his people. "The Oregon Country runs from here to the Pacific. So does all the water from here on."

The spring here was a big pool of alkali water in a setting of black mud, which supported a rank growth of wire grass. But nearby were two other springs, one boiling hot, the other cool and sweet, paradoxically coming out of the same rock formation. It was to the cold spring that Starbright led them, and there they made their camp.

The Wind River Mountains offered a new chance to hunt. Knowing that the wagon people would appreciate fresh meat, Starbright filled the last day by taking his own party northward. They raised deer and in late evening returned with all the meat they could carry on the pack horses. Starbright saw from the distance that the wagon train had not yet arrived.

Drawing closer to camp, he was surprised to see the shapes of two men waiting there. Leaving the pack string for the others to bring on, he rode ahead. He started to call a warm welcome, then the words died on his lips.

It was Lafferty and Wagner. Their expressions sent a chill through Starbright.

"Where's the wagons?" he asked Lafferty.

"Be here."

"Have trouble?"

Ralph Wagner pulled in a long breath, then let it out in the same slow way. "Yes, Starbright. We lost a girl yesterday."

"A girl?" Starbright could feel a pulse beating in his temples. "I only met one besides Rita, Doc. You don't mean —"

The Doctor nodded. "I'm afraid I do. It was Liz Templeton. The Indians got her."

Starbright sucked in a harsh breath. "Kill her?"

Wagner's eyes were bleak with something not good in a man of God. "No. They turned her loose. But it happened that Liz — Liz didn't want to come back."

The pass breeze stirred the sage, but Starbright couldn't hear it. His mind, shocked and sickened, refused to accept what he knew was true. The Lang party came in, caught the sense of things, and was silent. Starbright heard himself ask questions; he heard Lafferty give the answers, but unreality ran through it all.

"That girl's trouble," said Lafferty, "was she didn't know what it meant to be scared. She went where she pleased and when it pleased her. That's how it come to happen."

"Ah, no," said Starbright. "That's not why it happened."

"One night she just showed up missing," Lafferty went on. "People she traveled with got Doc and he got Redburn. Redburn got me. We hunted that night, but it was too dark by then. Next morning we found her where she'd gone to take a bath. Looked like she'd just crawled into the water and waited for it to drown her. Injuns didn't knock her cold and throw her in. Wasn't a mark on her except — except —" He couldn't continue.

"Try to catch the Injuns?" Starbright asked.

Lafferty shook his head. "Wasn't any use. Besides, it could have been a trick to get us to send out a party and leave the wagons weak. Only thing was to come on and forget it. If a man could. But we got to get back to the train. Redburn was anxious to know if you people made it. Wagons'll camp here, to-night."

"You don't need to go back," Starbright said. "I'm going. I want to see Redburn."

"Don't know how you could call it his fault," Lafferty said. "The thing just up and happened."

But Starbright rode out. He was thawing now and fury drove him. He came upon the wagons in the long pass in the early night. Tyre Redburn had seen a lone horseman approaching and had ridden forward. They came together well ahead of the train.

"It's you, Dix," Redburn gasped. "Is anything wrong?"

"Not on my end, damn you," Starbright returned. "But I heard how you paid off Walking Crow."

"Now, look," Redburn said desperately. "I couldn't have helped it. Walking Crow made a mistake. He got the wrong girl. I know how it happened. The day his brother visited the train I was talking to Liz Templeton. The Indian must have decided she was the one I was interested in."

"Ain't that dandy? Never cost you a thing, either. Your own girl's safe and sound. Alive and pure as a lily. I helped keep her that way. I wish to hell I hadn't."

"Why, damn you!" Redburn blazed. "Make it my fault, then! But I warned Liz Templeton time and again about going off alone the way she would. Especially to take a bath. Why, some scum in the train itself could have seen her and cut loose. We can't be sure that isn't what happened."

"You know better. He would have killed her. So would any stray Indians or white renegades who might have happened to see her. It was Walking Crow, and you know it. He turned her loose so she could get back and show you he'd carried out his revenge. Damn your black heart! You could have prevented it if you'd quit the train when I asked you. What do you think these people would do if they knew the truth about it?"

Redburn sucked in a sharp breath. "Will you tell them?"

"I came here to shoot you. But I think I'll help them hang you, instead."

89

The bluster left Redburn. In a pleading, almost pitiful way, he said, "Don't blame me too much. I made a mistake with The Pheasant. She made it easy, and I couldn't help myself. I didn't know she would take it the way she did. I didn't know Walking Crow would come back at me the way he did. Who can know it all? Who can always do the one right thing? Don't ruin me. I want to take these people through to the settlements. I want a new start out there. I want to marry Rita. You're right. They'd swing me on a wagon tongue if they knew. But what good would it do anybody, now?"

Something was sapping the bitter resolve in Starbright. It wasn't pity for Redburn, though the man was right in that the truth would not help the wagon company in any way. Walking Crow was appeased. The danger he had posed was behind. The hanging of Redburn would not bring back Liz Templeton. It would be a violence that the wagon people would regret to the day they died. Slowly Starbright put a brake on the impetus that had carried him here so violently.

After a moment, he said, "I'll keep my mouth shut. Not for your sake, but for the good of the company."

"Thanks."

"Goddamn you, don't give me your thanks! And walk wide of me from here on.

It strikes me that you might have been curious as to who got back from the hunt. We all did, Redburn, and left a pair of Missouri river rats buried out there. I smelled their ambush and spoiled it for them. Maybe I was to die. Maybe Kelly Lang. But it didn't come off."

"I don't know what you mean!" Redburn gasped.

"Then puzzle on it," said Redburn. The pilot wagons were pulling near. He swung his horse and rode back toward the springs.

He was slack, drained of feeling. Night had come on full. The yipping of coyotes carried in from the obscure distances. Their cry brought such an ineffable loneliness that Starbright's mind grew black with despair. He was thinking of Wagner, of the night he had seen that couple walk over the ridge hand in hand. Wagner was hit hard. It would not be well for him to know why Liz Templeton had died the way she did. Starbright knew that he had to seal his lips, at least for the present. . . .

There was a campfire at the springs. Rita and the men had cooked supper and tried to eat it. Now they sat about dispiritedly. Starbright briefly reported that the train would be there soon.

After a while Lang and the other men walked up the trail to meet the wagons. Rita had absented herself, and Starbright thought

91

at first that she had retired for the night. But presently she came back to the fire. The things between them privately were behind, swept away by the tragedy. Some of the repressed feeling broke in Starbright with an all but physical impact.

"Why are you scowling at me so?" Rita asked, surprised.

"So you figure on marrying Redburn," he mused. "It wouldn't be any good, Rita. Don't do it."

"Aren't you impertinent?" she asked.

"You're out of two different worlds," he went on stubbornly. "He's not rough and tough like me. It's another kind of difference. Just take it that you wouldn't like how he's lived or how he'll keep on living. Take my word for that."

A smile broke the severity of her mouth. "Would you say the same if you believed it was you I'm interested in. Certainly there were never two worlds any more different."

"I know that well." He lifted his head in sudden attention. Sound had carried forward on the stiffened breeze, telling him that the wagons were drawing near. He did not want to become a part of the camp for he had decided to be off long before the train was ready to go in the morning. Yet he didn't want to leave Rita alone here. He said, "Come with me while I make my camp. I'll bring you back when they get here."

"Crawling back in your hole?"

"I'm heading for Oregon in the morning." He was surprised at the veiled disappointment he thought he saw in her eyes. He attached little importance to that, yet was pleased to know she would regret his departure, even if it only meant the end of their game.

But Rita moved out of the firelight with him, subdued, different than he had known her to be before. He took his horses and packs forward for a quarter mile to get clear of the place where the wagons would circle.

"Where will you be in Oregon?" Rita asked finally.

"I'll ride till I find a hill where I can turn full circle and like all that I see. Then I'll claim it all for me and mine."

"Yours?" Rita said. "So you might mellow enough some day to have a family."

"I'm not hard."

"To my mind you thrive on brutality. You tried very hard to show me that."

The words, the memories, hit the canker in Starbright. The light of the stars fell upon her, showing him her clean young body with its healthy vitality, showing him also a picture of Liz Templeton as he had last seen her, laughing, happy! her hand in Wagner's.

This time Rita didn't back up when

Starbright moved toward her. "You're beautiful!" he breathed, and he dropped his hands roughly on her shoulders. "Pure as new snow — and no credit to you."

She stepped back, aghast. Then she turned and fled.

The great wagon train ground and rumbled in the near distance. It shaped itself into a tight circle, locked wagon tongue to hind standard. The Indian trouble had relieved the company of any tendency to complacency. Starbright was glad of that, at least. The Shoshone were mainly a peaceful people, but on ahead were the waspish Snakes.

Starbright smoked in the darkness for a long while before going to bed. His mind ran forward to the trail he would follow alone, through Forts Bridger, Hall, Boise, Walla Walla, and finally Vancouver. Packing, he would be more mobile and less subject to breakdowns, able to double the speed of the wagons. And yet alone, with a loneliness that was new to Dix Starbright.

In the late night Starbright's ears punched into his awareness some sound that he did not consciously hear. Training prevented his making any show of motion when he awakened. He opened his eyes and lay quietly, listening with hard intentness. The sagebrush about his camp was hip-high. He lay on his back, and instinct, rather than further warning, caused him to roll his head very slowly to the left.

A man rose up out of the sage but did not come to a full stand. He keenly regarded the place where Starbright lay in his blankets. The night light showed his shape, and it was the all but certain shape of Tyre Redburn. Still Starbright kept himself under rigid discipline, seeing in that instant that Redburn had decided not to trust his silence or else felt he'd been rendered more dangerous by the hint at Redburn's connection with the abortive ambush back on the desert.

Redburn came forward, step by slow step, as furtive and deadly as a Sioux. Starbright pulled in a slow, silent breath, bracing his body. He was certain that Redburn carried a knife, the silent steel of the underhanded. A knife — moccasin prints — they would make this seem the work of Indians.

Starbright wanted the man to pass beyond the point of turning back. Then Starbright would fight for his life, killing Redburn without compunction if he could. Such a struggle had been inherent in the situation from the start of the trouble. Waiting, Starbright accepted it.

The man's identity was beyond dispute as he prowled across the small open space of the campsite. At last he halted and Starbright, watching through slitted lids, saw hesitation enter the man and then be put down. If Redburn carried a knife he was concealing it behind his forearm, not wanting to betray his motive until the last moment. He came closer to Starbright, paused again. In that same instant Starbright sprang up at him, kicking aside the blankets as he rose.

Redburn let out a grunt of surprise but made no other sound. Swiftly he bent forward and struck in with his knife, driving it at Starbright's side. Starbright had not undressed when he retired. He lashed forward with a moccasined foot, driving his ankle hard into Redburn's crotch, twisting away from the swing of the knife. The blade ripped his buckskin shirt but flashed on in its arc. Pain drove Redburn backward, and Starbright was on him in full assault.

Starbright drove blows to the belly, head, and chest of the stunned man. Redburn's big body and powerful legs held him up. He kept hold of his knife, and when the sick paralysis had left him he stiffened an arm to hold Starbright away. Then he grabbed at Starbright with his free hand and lifted the knife to drive it again.

Starbright side-stepped the weapon and this time caught the arm that drove it. He made a quick, full turn, getting a shoulder in Redburn's armpit, swinging on and bending forward in a way that whipped the man up and across his back. Redburn came down full length with an impact that would have knocked a frailer man senseless. Starbright's quick, ruthless wristlock released the knife in the man's stubborn grip. Starbright bent and picked the weapon up, tossing it into the sage.

"Now, fight a man's fight!" he gasped.

Redburn rolled onto his belly and tried to push up. He did not make an outcry, and Starbright wanted neither help nor audience in what he meant to do. On the second try, Redburn came to his feet. He spread his arms and lunged in quickly, wanting to grapple. Starbright hit him, swift and hard, his knuckles smashing Redburn's lips. Redburn came on. Starbright struck out again, a heavy body blow that failed to stop the man.

Redburn cocked his fist and threw a sudden overhand punch. It caught Starbright on the thrust of his own drive. It snapped back his head, and before he could rebaiance himself Redburn had slugged him hard in the belly. The man's hatred was now mixed with fear. His original hope seemed forgotten. Like Starbright, he wanted to fight it out. He came forward, arms swinging, fists landing up and down Starbright's chest and belly.

Starbright might have weathered it had not a scattered blanket tangled his feet. He went down and Redburn was on him, sensing victory, keeping up a gurgling grunt with his blows. With a hard heave, Starbright rolled and suddenly found himself on top. He gagged for breath, and the numbness of his flesh, the slow response of his muscles told him he was hurt. He hit Redburn twice, three times, then rolled clear.

For a second he thought that Redburn wasn't going to try to get up. Then the man made a sudden move and came to his feet.

In a strange, strangled whisper Redburn said, "Sooner or later it had to be. You know too much. You guess too much." It was dispassionate, a statement of fact, a declaration, and in its way a justification. Fists ready to strike, he charged again.

Starbright met him head-on. He stood and fought back. His paralysis seemed to deepen, to spread all through him. Each massive blow from Redburn jarred him but didn't seem to cause pain. The thud of his own fists was all that told him he was hitting with power, himself.

His killing rage increased. Slowly he drove Redburn out of the open and into the sage. Then it was Redburn's turn to tangle on the underfooting. He fell heavily. He got half up before Starbright flattened him again. Redburn grabbed his legs, bringing Starbright down on him. They rolled over, and over. Starbright got his fingers in Redburn's hair, and each time he came on top he smashed the man's head against the earth. All at once Redburn quit twisting and struggling. But Starbright kept on slamming his head.

It dawned on him finally that he was wooling an unconscious man. He grew motionless, but for long moments sat astride Redburn, his chest heaving, his legs refusing to lift him up. At last he rolled off and lay on his side. He hadn't killed Redburn, and it wasn't in him to kill an unconscious man. So Starbright's victory was mixed with regret.

CHAPTER SEVEN

It seemed forever before Starbright could get to his feet. He grew aware that the sweat bathing him was mixed with blood, his own blended with Redburn's. The man lay in complete exhaustion on the sandy earth, partly under a sagebush. A slow breath gurgled in his pulpy nose. Five minutes later he still had made no other movement.

Starbright let out a sigh. Reaction roiled in him, a shaking aversion to the violence that still drove him heedlessly. He didn't want to touch Redburn again, but he made himself bend and get the man up and across his shoulders. He went lurching along the trail toward the wagon camp.

He was within hailing distance before he saw sign of the night guard, who sent out a ripping challenge.

"Who's that?"

"Starbright. Man hurt. Get Doc Wagner and send him to Redburn's wagon."

"I better help," the guard said, running forward. "Redburn's wagon ain't far from the Doc's."

Starbright held onto his ugly burden, but the guard's guidance saved him weary steps.

They reached a wagon where the night guard roused Redburn's campmate, Cob Boze. The Missouri tough took one look at what Starbright carried and cursed.

"Injuns do it?" Boze gasped.

"He ran into the edge of a door," said Starbright. "Spread some blankets, damn you, or get a basket I can put him in. I'm sick and tired of his smell."

"You done it!" Boze snarled, his eyes glimmering at Starbright.

"That's right," said Starbright. "And so far I've killed three of your breed, Boze. You going to be next?"

"What you got against me?" Boze sputtered.

"Same thing I've got against any skunk."

"By God!" Boze exploded. "Was I you, I wouldn't be so cocky! Your day's comin'! You ain't always going to be such a fool for luck!"

"If you ain't going to lay out bedding," said Starbright, "he'll have to make do with the ground." He dumped his load, wheeled and strode back into the night.

He slept no more. The wheeling stars told him that daylight was not far off. There was enough starlight to tempt him to pack his camp and be off. But there would be questions, a natural curiosity in the wagon company about the terrible fight. Though Starbright had no ready answers, he did not mean to run away from the inquiry. He sat stolidly by his packs, stiff and aching. Then at last the day's dawning shone in the sky.

Starbright roused himself out of stupor. Rising, he emptied one of his big canteens into a kettle and scrubbed the blood and grime from himself. He had used up his last clean buckskins, and those he wore were filthy and torn. But he let it go at that and started his breakfast fire.

He wasn't surprised to see the visitor who appeared between him and the wagon camp, but the arrival of Ralph Wagner puzzled Starbright at first. There was a queer expression on the doctor's lean face, something that had never been there before. Wagner stopped at the edge of the sage, bent from sight, then rose into view again. He paused again before he came up to Starbright, regarding the signs of violence on the scuffed earth and on Starbright himself.

Then Starbright gave a start. Wagner carried a knife, which he had picked up when he bent down.

"What's this?" he asked. It was a stranger's voice, roughened yet quiet.

"Looks like a hunting knife," Starbright answered.

"What was it doing there?"

"Maybe somebody lost it. Been thousands of people camped here."

Wagner shook his head. "Thousands of people didn't lose it. Just one man. And he's all but dead for his pains. What was the trouble over, Starbright? You two were on speaking terms at the Platte crossing. Now you try to kill each other. About something between there and here?" There was a flat and crowding suspicion in the doctor's voice. He was putting it together; he was adding it up. He sensed that this moment and the moment of Liz Templeton's ruin were directly connected. And there was incipient violence in the man of God.

"Easy, Doc," said Starbright. "Men fight for a lot of reasons. What's Redburn's account of it?"

"He's not making one. He's still unconscious. I think you've killed him, Starbright. But maybe not. Only time will tell." Wagner's eyes burned into Starbright's. "I want to know why you fought."

"It was an old grudge. Redburn wanted it settled before I pull on ahead. It got settled."

Wagner lifted an eyebrow. "How did he happen to lose his knife?"

"Is it his?"

"You know it is."

"Then you better forget you saw it, Doc. Men fighting ain't important. Getting this company over this trail is. Redburn's its captain, and he's done all right at that. Throw that sticker away and rub it out of your mind."

"So he did try to murder you," Wagner

said. He was lost in thought for a moment, then abruptly he tossed the hunting knife to the earth at Starbright's feet. "Redburn's not likely to lead the train again, Starbright. He'll either be a corpse or a cripple. The company is already short a leader. You're responsible for that, even if it was brought to you."

"Meaning what?"

"You've got to take over the job."

"Hell I do!" Starbright snapped. "If Redburn can't cut it, there's Lafferty. He aims to stick with the train. He's had as much experience as me and more than Redburn."

"He's not the forceful personality a train captain's got to be. Besides that, he's too hot-headed and ready for a fight. You're the man."

"Not me," said Starbright.

The doctor turned and walked away. Starbright watched the thin shoulders fade in the distance to be lost in the sage. Then he took Redburn's knife and buried it in the sand, afterward brushing out the traces of fresh digging. But he didn't get his horses to pack up, just yet. He saw Kelly Lang coming toward his camp.

There was an aggressive swing to Lang's body. As he came up, his face was set. Watching the approach, Starbright wondered if Rita at last had confided in her father, turned vindictive by the incident of the previous night. The mountain man squared his sore shoulders, wondering if he had another fight to face.

Lang came up briskly, merely nodding. He said, "Starbright, I want you to take me back. At least as far as Fort Laramie. As far as the Missouri, if you will."

"Why?" Starbright gasped.

"I've got men to catch and kill," said Lang bitterly. "God help me, I'll do it. It was everything I had in the world. I trusted them!"

"Who you talking about, man?"

"Ah," said Lang. "You haven't heard. Two of my men deserted my wagons while we were hunting. They broke open my chest and stole my gold. They killed the other man I left behind. Damn their black hearts! I'll catch them, Starbright, and when I do they'll pay for it!"

Starbright shook his head. "Maybe not. You'll never find them. Or if you did, they'd already be dead. Lang, they're likely buried between here and where we left the train. They never betrayed you, not the two who're missing."

"What in hell are you getting at?"

"Tell me your part first."

Lang's account of his shaking misfortune was brief. His wagons had arrived here the night before, driven by men from the main company. They had told him what had happened. The morning after the first camp this side of the Platte crossing, his personal servant had been found dead in his blankets, a knife in his heart. The two other men left with the wagons had vanished. Redburn, when called in, discovered that the chest had been broken open and rifled. That was all.

"You talk to Redburn?" Starbright asked narrowly.

Kelly Lang shook his head. "I didn't get a chance last night. Now the Doctor tells me I might never get one. I'm waiting to hear why you said what you did about my men being dead."

"Just my hunch," Starbright said bitterly. "And I think you were to have been killed in the ambush we escaped on the desert."

"But why?"

"You know the old shell game. One's got the pea under it — the other ain't. And the shells are in cunning hands. Your busted chest could be one shell. Somebody else has got the other. Maybe the pea's been switched so quick nobody could guess where it went. If he didn't know other things to make him wonder?"

"You know?"

"I could make a good guess," the buckskin man answered. "Lang, since you didn't die the way it was planned you should, the worst thing you could do now would be to head East now hunting that gold. That might suit somebody fine. Provided you left your daughter for him to enjoy with your gold."

"You mean Redburn." For a while Lang was silent. "I guessed at Laramie that you were suspicious of him. I think I've got a right to know why."

"You have," Starbright agreed. "Tell me of your dealings with him."

Again Lang talked quietly. He had met Redburn only a few months before taking to the trail. He had been greatly impressed by the fellow. According to Redburn, he had made a fortune in the fur trade. He was going to Oregon to put his capital to constructive use in developing the country. He had got Lang interested in the same kind of venture for himself.

Lang was not an extremely wealthy man. He had converted everything he possessed into gold since the new settlements had no banking facilities whatsoever. It amounted to some sixty thousand dollars, all of which had now vanished. Apparently it had not leaked out that Redburn was transporting an equal sum in his own wagon. Once in Oregon City, they meant to start a bank as equal partners.

"And, there you have it," said Starbright. "Lang, you stick with the train. Your gold's still here and in Redburn's wagon. I take it you couldn't identify the stuff."

"Coin of the realm," Lang said, shaking his head.

"You could search his wagon and find the gold. But, if he could talk, he'd claim it was only the sixty thousand he was fetching out. See what I meant? The pea's just moved from the full shell to the empty one."

"You could be right, Starbright," Lang admitted.

"I know I am. Now that you know, stick with the train. If he lives, don't let him know you're suspicious. You'll get your share of the breaks."

"A thief and murderer!" Lang said. "Starbright, I could use your help. Join my party."

Starbright shook his head. "If you can't handle Redburn, now that you know about him, you'll never make out in this country."

An angry look flashed in Lang's eyes. "I didn't mean that, damn you. It's Rita. Redburn's captured her fancy. So have you, but you're going away while Redburn dances attendance. That worries me."

"She's grown."

"And mule-headed. If I told her what I now believe about Redburn and that it came from you, it would only set her in his defense. Let me try to break them up, and she'd marry him instantly. I know Rita.

She's over at his wagon right now, playing nurse."

Starbright stared, then snapped, "Let her."

Yet he still did not break camp after Lang went back to the wagon company. The Pheasant — Liz Templeton — that was one cycle that had come full circle and was now a thing of the past. A new conflict had risen and it filled Starbright's thoughts, giving direction and meaning to the trail yet ahead.

The talk with Lang had clarified matters, settling Starbright's mind. Redburn's hidden motive in all this venture was devilishly simple and clever. By pretending to bring a matching amount of gold West to go into business with Kelly Lang, Redburn had prepared a basis for his crime. All he needed to do, thereafter, was get Lang's gold into his own possession and see that somehow Lang died. He could then have Rita and a sudden wealth she would believe to have been his all along. The trail had afforded excellent opportunities for carrying out his plans.

Redburn had hired the Missouri toughs to lurk in the vicinity of the train and act as chance afforded. Starbright now understood that he himself had upset Redburn's first effort to pull it off when he had first seen the Langs on the far side of Fort Laramie. Redburn's swift mind had seen a second chance in the plan to switch Rita swiftly across the divide in the guise of a hunting trip. His henchmen had failed to do away with Lang, but Redburn had got hold of the gold.

Therefore, Lang was still in mortal danger if Redburn lived. Cob Boze was a henchman also, still on hand, while Starbright had the strong feeling it had been his or Redburn's knife that had done for Lang's hired men.

At noon the big wagon train was still encamped, and Starbright had not departed. The loose stock herd had been moved on the Pacific Creek for water and grass. Occasionally somebody passed close to the lone camp, but nobody approached him. Starbright knew he was on trial with the company. Wagner probably had given out the account Starbright had given that it had been personal ill will degenerating into a brawl. But Redburn had shown his people nothing but competence and a durable good humor. It was obvious that the settlers' sympathy lay with him, if for no other reason than that Redburn was known to them while Starbright had been a detached, tough-acting stranger to them.

Shortly after midday, Starbright walked up to the wagon camp. He found Wagner at Redburn's wagon; he also found Rita there. The quick, loathing way she looked at him told Starbright that he had damned himself with her, not only by what he had said to her the night before but through the merciless whipping of Redburn.

"How is he?" Starbright asked Wagner.

"Better than I expected. He's regained consciousness."

"Could he stand traveling?"

"It wouldn't matter much."

"I'll lead you to Fort Bridger," Starbright said regretfully. "If Redburn can't take over there, you'll find somebody else at the fort who can. We'll start tomorrow morning on one condition — that the people endorse it. I'll take no responsibility without their full consent."

"Good enough." Wagner smiled slightly. "I'll tell them. They're scattered now, but we'll have a meeting this evening. You be there."

"Be around."

Rita was not looking at them or showing any outward interest in the talk. Starbright stared at her in a blunt and brittle anger.

"What's Redburn say about the rumpus?" he asked.

"What you did," Wagner answered. "That it was a personal thing that had to be settled and got settled."

"You don't accept that?" Starbright asked Rita.

She looked fully at him then, and Starbright was disturbed by the contempt in her eyes. "Up to a certain point. Beyond that point it was nothing but sheer brutality. Some men would have stopped with whipping him. You went on to ruin him."

"Easy, Rita," said Wagner. "Maybe there are things you don't understand."

"I understand enough."

"I wonder," Wagner said, and his steady gaze made her turn her back on them.

It was with reluctance that Starbright returned to the wagon camp again that evening to attend the meeting of the settlers. He saw from their cold faces that they knew the reason for the general assembly. He saw their distrust of him, in many cases their open dislike. Redburn had been popular and now received, in addition, the sympathy that always went to the underdog. Starbright's jaws bulged more prominently.

He mounted a wagon tongue, thrust his thumbs under his belt, and said, "I don't give a damn what you think. I don't care whether you get a mile past Fort Bridger. But I admit I had something to do with nailing you down here. I feel a responsibility to get you that far. I'll meet it if you want. But I'll be damned if I'll go a step with you without your full consent."

Kelly Lang stood near, watching puzzledly, yet with a vague satisfaction in his eyes. He said, "You needn't be so tough about it, friend. Of course we consent. And I make the motion that we elect you captain *pro temp.*" The man's smart, smooth assist at that point turned the trick.

Wagner, acting as chairman, called for a second to the motion and got it. It went on through to a subdued but unanimous vote for Starbright. The settlers had little choice. They had to have a leader who understood the country and its requirements. Redburn was helpless, and Lafferty lacked the stature of leadership.

"All right," said Starbright. "We'll go in the morning."

CHAPTER EIGHT

The camp broke up at dawn, the wagons rolled on. Starbright found a lad to handle his pack animals, leaving him free to move about. The promise of renewed trailing was a tonic to the company. Gravity left it, and with that a great deal of the coldness that had been shown the mountain man. Yet there had been a galling note for him when Rita openly joined Redburn's wagon to travel with it and take care of the hurt man. It was as Kelly Lang had forewarned. Redburn in defeat roused her sympathies, while Starbright in victory drew forth from her the full force of her violent antipathies.

The miles, the days fell behind. Starbright had mainly to point out the way, to pick campsites and set the march, to be an experienced man on hand in case of need. The country was of a nature to hold all minds to immediate circumstances. The sagebrush plateaus of the pass fell behind. Down the length of Pacific Creek, while the land dropped away, down at last to the Little Sandy crossing and on to Big Sand and the desert march to Green River.

Starbright made the last trek at night, a

distance of some thirty-five miles in which there was scarcely a blade of grass and not a drop of water. But he laughed at the settlers' forebodings. "Wait till you see the cut-rock desert," he told them. "That's four-hundred-miles long. Snake Injuns all the way. Yet that's just the start of the rough country."

The crossing of Green River was not difficult. The stream ran over colored shale that gave it the name. It was large, limpid, and cool. Cottonwood stood along its bank, with grass greening there. In spite of the hurry driving him, Starbright understood the relief of the company in being reprieved even briefly from the vast desert. He ordered a day's layover to soak wheel rims, make repairs, and allow rest to the punished people and even more sorely abused livestock.

By then Starbright had accepted Wagner's invitation to attach himself to his wagon. On the evening when they reached Green River, the doctor put an unexpected question to the mountain man. They were seated at their supper fire, the meal eaten, smoking their pipes.

"Dix," Wagner said abruptly, "do you have any religious feeling?"

"No," said Starbright.

"You're a liar. You've got a great sympathy for people behind that granite front. You've got respect for nature, a reverence for life."

"That's religion?"

"It'll do to start with."

"Let me ask one," said Starbright. "Say you met the man you knew to be responsible for what happened on the Sweetwater. What would you do?"

"I'd kill him."

"Then I got religion, too," said Starbright.

The next day saw a quietly busy camp. The wagons had rolled steadily since the pass and this was the first real rest. Children sprang into renewed life, full of natural exuberance. The men, the women eased up out of longing and the necessity for taking respite where it came. The water essential to a happy camp was here, as was the shade. The stock was moved forward again and left under guard.

Women seized the opportunity to wash clothes. They got out their iron skillets and kettles to cook for today and days ahead. Men looked to their stock and wagons. They flung private, speculative glances at the forward trail.

With only a pack outfit to worry over, Starbright found himself at loose ends. He was still without a sense of intimacy with the company. He kept aloof from all but Wagner and Lang. The doctor was not vocal company very often, any more. He was growing as silent as Starbright. This day he went off alone down the river.

He was wrestling with something within him, and whenever Starbright recalled how Wagner had sought to help the man who had put the unhealable hurt within himself, his hatred of Tyre Redburn mounted.

Starbright was whittling at his camp when Rita appeared finally. Starbright looked up in surprise for he had seen little of her since he had taken over the company. Her manner had changed, he thought. The stubborn hostility seemed less, and he sensed in her now a timid sort of uncertainty.

She did not acknowledge his nod, only saying, "Tyre would like for you to come over to his wagon."

"What in tunket for?" Starbright asked, astounded.

"Not to quarrel. I wish you'd do it."

Starbright scowled and saw earnestness in her eyes. She looked tired. He knew that she had devoted herself to the hurt man without stint. "All right. Since it's you that's asking."

He walked with her to the Redburn wagon. He was surprised to discover that Redburn was dressed and sitting on a blanket on the ground. His face was almost healed, but he had lost weight. He sat in a twisted way, as if seeking comfort for his body and not finding it. Cob Boze was not around.

Redburn glanced at Starbright, then at

Rita, who had started to move away.

"Don't leave," he told her. "You know what I'm going to say. Starbright, I apologize. I told Rita it was my fault. I nursed an old grudge from the old days and finally lost my head."

"Don't give a hoot in hell what you told her. What do you want of me?"

"I want you to forget it."

Starbright could only stare. He had long since learned to listen to the quality of a man's voice. Redburn's sounded sincere, and he looked sincere. Rita was smiling, in combined relief and pride, at Redburn. Starbright had a feeling that she had urged him to do this — or that Redburn was well enough to look ahead and want to mend his fences.

"Then," Starbright said, "if you're ready to take over the train, I'll pack on."

"I'm not ready. Wagner says I might never be ready. I couldn't sit a saddle right now if my life depended on it. The job's yours."

"I agreed to take it only as far as Bridger." Starbright was shocked by Redburn's statement. There was no outward resentment in Redburn, not a trace. Yet this was foreign to the man's nature, his past. Therefore this new attitude was feigned, or had come only at the prompting of Rita. Starbright looked at her. "He tell you what that grudge was?"

She shook her head. "No, and I don't want to know. He apologized. Are you man enough to accept it? I'd like you better if you would. I'd be ready to drop my own quarrel without your apology."

Starbright blinked, finding himself drawn farther and farther beyond his comprehension. She sounded as if she were offering a resumed friendship as a bribe. Either she cared a great deal for Redburn and wanted to restore him to his place in the company and his own self-esteem, or she had something else in her mind that she — or both of them — were keeping hidden.

Starbright said, "I'll take the company to Fort Bridger, as agreed."

"And about that," Redburn said quickly. "I'm not trying to tell you how to run this train, but I have a suggestion. We could save ourselves a week's time if we passed Bridger up. There's that old trapper trail that runs from here to Hams Fork. Wagons used it before Jim Bridger built his post. It would lop forty or fifty miles off for us. I had it in mind when I thought I would be leading the train through here. We've made good time from Laramie, and we're not short of provisions. Why not strike straight from here to Fort Hall?"

Starbright rubbed his chin. He was aware of the cutoff, a stretch that originally had been the main overland trail. Then Jim Bridger had built his fort a distance to the south. The emigrants had changed the route to take advantage of the chance to obtain provisions and repairs. What Redburn suggested was true and sensible. It would save the settlers considerable trudging and valuable time.

"Put it up to the people," Redburn urged. "They'll take to the idea."

"Maybe I will," Starbright said.

He went back to his own camp with suspicion nagging at his mind. He thought he knew why Redburn wanted to avoid Fort Bridges. The forts ahead were British. Bridges was the last such American outpost before the Willamette settlements. There was little exchange course between the two fur interests. Bridges would be the last place where there was apt to be mountain men able to verify the story Starbright and Lafferty could tell of Redburn's past. So Redburn's apology was expedient and not sincere, whatever Rita's reason for being pleased about it.

Starbright explained the possibility to the wagon company that evening. They were more than agreeable. A mile of trail was a mile of walking for the men and older boys, a mile of dust and punishment as the country steadily worsened. Forty miles was a tremendous gain, and thus it was that the next morning the wagons headed west instead of continuing south as had been planned.

There was satisfaction in Starbright's

work now, reluctant though he was to admit it. The train in motion was a stirring sight. Every one of the seventy-two wagons that had left the Missouri was still in the dusty, drawnout line of march. The vehicles groaned and rumbled but kept on and on, a mile between the pilot wagons and the unfortunates in the rear. Men tramped beside their vehicles, faces caked with dust, the dust runneled with sweat, across their sloped shoulders a bullwhack or a rifle. Children released excess energies by darting on either side of the line, the inevitable dogs bounding with them. The march went forward until noon each day, when a halt was made for a quick meal without the teams being unhooked, and then it went on again until sunset. Each day it moved westward with the sun.

The first day put the caravan to Hams Fork, the second and third carried it past the northern tip of the Bear River range. Abruptly the trail bent north, along the Bear itself. Another day and the wagons followed the Bear into the lifts of the Salt River Mountains. Fort Hall drew ever nearer, and spirits soared high. And with all this, there was a quiet and personal satisfaction for Starbright. With Redburn up and able to get along with the help of his man Boze, Rita returned to Kelly Lang's big wagon.

Starbright was making a discovery that all but had him beat. His life had held little of the luxury of women. It startled and bewildered him when his temper subsided enough to reveal how much Rita had come to mean to him. He had known women of physical appeal before. On occasions he had possessed them transiently. Now that Rita seemed to have dropped her own hostility, he felt his hunger for her strongly. It was a torture to remember what she might have given him that night at Monohan's camp. What he had sacrificed to gain a triumph over her.

Three more days through the valley of the Bear, and Starbright's wagons reached Soda Springs. Strongly mineral, the water was usable, with the springs scattered on a wheeling, treeless flat. Except for trails worn to them by Indians and white men, the springs would have been lost in the sage. Naked hills ran all about the flat except at the water gaps, forbidding barriers in a hot land that had only these effervescent waters to offer a passer-by.

Starbright realized that rest was more a necessity than a luxury at this stage of the crossing. His order for another day's layover was received gratefully.

Starbright wasn't greatly surprised when Kelly Lang sought him out while the camps were being set up. Lang said, "Dix, come over and have supper with us."

Starbright eyed him. "What you fishing for now?"

"I still want a good man on my side. How about it?"

"All right, I will. And thanks."

He was excited, yet turned weak with stage fright. Supper would bring him face to face with Rita for the first time since their quarrel, except for the occasions when Redburn had been on hand.

Ralph Wagner was faintly amused but said nothing when Starbright announced casually that he would not be on hand for supper. Without immediate comment, Wagner went on cooking his own supper.

He made his only remark when Starbright departed. "Remember, I'm a preacher. I've already married some couples in this company."

"You go to hell," said Starbright.

He took his time walking over to the Lang camp. Kelly Lang had lost his servants and his money, but he still had the big wagon with its lavish equipment and supplies. The table under the canvas fly was set with a cloth and full dinner service. Rita was cooking the meal and looked competent, Starbright noted. She was alone.

"Dad went off to hunt a spring," she said. "He's wondering if this water here would make a decent whisky and soda."

"Well, there's plenty of water," said Starbright. "If he's got the whisky."

"Got it and hitting it too hard lately."

"Man who's lost sixty thousand's got a right. Man who's been betrayed's got a double right. But I think it's mainly to help him bide his time."

"Bide his time," Rita said. "For what?"

"Till he gets his gold back and squares it with the man who's got it."

"By now," said Rita, "his gold is probably back East."

Lang came in then, carrying a pail of water. Rummaging in a wagon locker, he brought forth a bottle of whisky. They had a drink while Rita put supper on the table. Starbright did not like the concoction, but Lang seemed to figure he had brought a touch of civilization to the wild desert country.

CHAPTER NINE

Starbright lazed about the wagon camp all through the next day. The hunting party that had gone forth in the morning returned at dusk, arousing excitement with two mule-deer carcasses. The division of the meat among so many people made it spread thin, but it was fresh meat and many pots had waited and it soon disappeared.

Then, in the moonlight, came the first dance the company had felt like having since the death of Liz Templeton. Somewhere a fiddle cried out, an accordion joining it. Presently a banjo and a mouth harp were added. From scores of supper fires, people rose up to listen. To listen was to start moving toward the source of the music, which was across the train from Wagner's wagon.

Starbright, feeling the excitement, looked closely at Wagner. The doctor had lifted his head in interest.

"Let's go, Doc," Starbright said.

"Tired, Dix. Rather go to bed."

Starbright frowned at him. Wagner was turning into a recluse except when his profession forced him to mingle. He was nursing his grief, letting it gnaw at his inwards. Starbright walked off by himself, crossing the wagon circle.

The dancing had begun, the musicians sitting in the firelight and pleased with their drawing power. A caller's voice was loud, "Hands in your pockets . . . backs to the wall . . . chew your tobaccer . . . and balance all!" Couples had already started a quadrille, with more running hand in hand to get into it.

Starbright saw Lafferty, then he spotted Rita. She was being pulled into the dance by a good-looking young settler in homespun. But she liked it and was laughing, her hair tumbling and her eyes ashine. Starbright began to sidle his way forward through the press.

"Honor your partner and don't be afraid! Swing on the corners with a waltz promenade!"

It was then that Starbright saw Tyre Redburn standing on a pair of whittled canes. The man had been getting about for several days, forcing himself to walk beside his wagon as if willing strength and use back into his wasted big frame. His trouble now was only a dragging leg and a slow-moving arm. Starbright came up at his side and Redburn didn't notice him.

The man was watching Rita closely and with a steady hunger.

Starbright said, "Redburn, how are you making out?"

Redburn swung quickly and frowned, saying, "I'm making out."

"Fork a horse pretty soon?"

After a long study, Redburn said, "Starbright, what I said the other day I had to say. But I'd as soon not have your solicitousness about me."

Starbright frowned as he walked on. He had been extremely suspicious about Redburn's contrition. He understood what had finally brought the spilling truculence out of him. Redburn was not one to like the sidelines in a thing like this dance. He did not like the sight of Rita dancing in the arms of a strapping, able-bodied young settler. There was a blood clot on Redburn's brain, Wagner had said. If it dissolved, the man might recover. If not, he would remain crippled in spite of his driving will. Redburn had been told that, and he still hated the man who had visited it upon him.

A swinging anger of his own showed in Starbright's stride. The music broke at that moment but he headed on, straight toward Rita. She looked surprised as he brushed up to her through several eager young men. The music started again in a lively rigadoon. A settler reached for the girl, but Starbright stepped between.

"Come with me," he said to Rita.

"Something wrong?" she asked sharply.

"Plenty."

She came along with him, puzzled and hustling to keep up with his determined stride. He moved out of the crowd and on down the bending line of wagons. When the vehicles had cut them from the sight of the dance, he halted at one whose occupants were gone. He turned to face her.

"Before I shot off my face at Pacific Springs," he said gruffly, "you showed signs of liking me. You sounded as if you wanted to see me again on the Willamette. I never made an apology for the rotten thing I said that night. I make it now. Something was eating me bad, that night. Something you never understood. I'm sorry. I'll bend over if you want to deliver a kick."

"Why, Dix. What's got into you?"

"I reckon I love you," he said miserably. "I wanted you to know it before I quit the train. Which I will at Fort Hall. I hope you'll still want to see me on the Willamette. I hope you'll still be free for me to seek you."

Rita laughed softly. "Remember the other time we slipped away from a dance? And the night at Johnny's camp?"

"I regret both times," he said.

She faced him, her face lifted, the starlight reflected in her eyes. He was afraid now of the roughness that could on occasion seize him. He touched her cheeks gently with his hands. Then her palms touched against his sides, and he seized her. She was limp against him, her lips stirring beneath his for a long moment.

"Let me go now," she whispered. "But I wanted you to have that. I want you to carry it with you."

"Every step to the valley."

"And all your life."

"No doubt of that."

"Fine," she said. "Now I'll tell you of my own plans for Fort Hall, Dix Starbright. When we reach there, Tyre and I will have Doctor Wagner marry us." Laughing, she slipped past him and ran back toward the dance.

Starbright knew that he had it coming. He had hit her hard, twice in a row and without mercy. So he deserved to have this searing flame in his flesh, kindled by her kiss, by the yielding long pressure of her body. She had the right to make a new move in their little game, a game he had secretly hoped she had abandoned.

The fire in Starbright took on its taint of anger. It roared on to become his old and heedless antagonism toward her. He didn't try to analyze the feeling, to pick out the splinters of shattered pride or to expose the festers of raw jealousy of Tyre Redburn. Let her marry the man and find out for herself what her wilfulness had brought her. Let her father die, murdered by the lover who already had stolen his gold. It was no concern of Starbright's.

The wagon train moved on in the early dawn, crossing the hills to the edge of the great Snake River plain, then bending down to Fort Hall. The march required nearly a week of rough going, days of punishment for the company, days of dread for Starbright.

On the last night, Kelly Lang sought Starbright, saying, "Rita told me last night what she says she told you a week back. It can't happen. Not if I have to kill Redburn to stop it."

"She of age?" Starbright asked.

Lang nodded. "And she won't believe a thing I say. She holds you responsible for poisoning my mind against Redburn. She'll marry him, Starbright, unless I get rough."

"Then get rough. I don't care."

"You're a damned liar," said Lang, and he walked away.

Fort Hall was a Hudson's Bay Company outpost. It flew the H B C red-lettered flag that meant, according to the American trappers, "Here before Christ." Starbright had never visited it before. He judged that it covered about half an acre. Its thick walls were only shoulder-high to a tall man. Within the stockade were the usual trading rooms, storehouses, and dwellings. There was a two-story bastion.

The arriving train created excitement at the fort as it had at Fort Laramie. Trappers rode out to welcome the company, to have a look at its women. They spotted Starbright in his buckskins and made cautious overtures. They had been rivals, but Starbright had put those days behind and was friendly.

They showed him where to camp, between the river and the fort, and where to put the herd for the best grazing. As soon as that was done, the settlers swarmed over the fort, eager for supplies, some of them to hunt up mechanics. Starbright's job was done. He felt no relief and even less satisfaction.

But the wedding apparently was to be a surprise. Starbright had heard no rumor of it in the big party, had been too proud to inquire of Wagner about the arrangements. He made his last camp with Wagner, expecting to hit the trail alone at dawn. He knew he was apt to kill Tyre Redburn if he stayed here another day.

One of the fort's subfactors sought Starbright that evening. He said, "I hope you people are turning off here for California. That's about the only way you can go, unless you turn back where you came from."

Starbright asked, "What's wrong with the Oregon Trail?"

"Drought. We've had the driest year in my

memory. You're the fourth train that's come by this season, and the largest. You couldn't find grass for a herd like yours within fifty miles of the trail. I know. I came through from Fort Boise last week. You won't make it to the Colorado. There just isn't the grass."

Wagner looked up at Starbright and said, "Going to desert us in a situation like this? I don't want to go to California. I don't want to go back where I came from. And I don't think anybody else in this company feels any different."

"What can I do, man? Grow you a new crop of grass?"

"No, Dix. But what do we do?"

"Drop the livestock."

"And pull the wagons ourselves?"

Starbright sighed. "Oh, hell. But I've been worried. It's drier than I figured to find it out here. These people had better go to California."

"They don't want to. You don't. Why should they be any more willing to change their whole plan?"

"Damn it," said Starbright, "there's another way. I was over it once when I guided some fellows to the Columbia. Runs north of here, over against the Salmon Mountains. It's only a pack trail. Trappers use it and Injuns. Plenty of water and grass."

The next morning Starbright went up to the fort and talked to others there. They all confirmed the first man's opinion. The cutrock desert to the west would be a death trap for a train as big as this. The California trail was still good. There was a man there willing to take Starbright's place and guide the train to the Sacramento. They were aghast when he mentioned the trapper trail that ran through to the north.

"You'd never get wagons over it," a man said.

Starbright flicked him a cool glance. "Anybody ever try? No? Then how do you know?"

It was becoming a challenge to him, even though he realized it would again involve him deeply with the wagon company, a company that was going to embrace Rita as Redburn's bride.

There was only one man, a listening trapper, who seemed inclined to agree with him. Finally that man said, "Maybe it could be done, boys. Be plenty of rough going, for fair. Locking and roping and doubling on the hills. Clearing and grading and a man cussin' hisself blue for havin' picked it. But he might get himself through."

That decided it for Starbright. He knew he was going to propose it to the wagon company.

Another day passed without a wedding or even the rumor of one. Still Starbright could not bring himself to ask Wagner when it was to be. But such an event, known in advance,

133

would cause excitement to leap through the train. That had not happened. Instead, gloom had settled heavily on the big company.

The people had heard the talk about the drought trail that lay before them — that or the alternative of turning off for California. But they wanted Oregon; they had dreamed of Oregon, and that was where they still wanted to go. At last Starbright spread the word that a meeting would be held.

In the gathering twilight he faced a great ring of people gathered at his camp. He said, "If you want to go with me, I'll take you by a new way to Oregon. A new trail when it comes to wagons, though there's been trappers over it for years, Injuns for centuries. But it hasn't been grazed off, it ain't droughted off. There'd be water and grass to spare."

"What about Injuns?" a man said. "Feller said it's right through the heart of their hunting country. Said they'd put on their war paint if we come through. He was set strong against your notion, Starbright."

"It's a way to Oregon, if you want to get there, friend."

Questions came at him, which he answered truthfully. It would be tough but no tougher than the grassless cutrock desert. It would be farther and slower because it was unbroken by wagons. But the country would sustain their herd. They would take emergency materials from the fort, plenty of iron and rope. Yes, and gun powder and lead because it was true about Indians. They were Snakes. They were mean. They were apt to consider the passage an outrageous violation of their private domain. Thus, making no promises except the chance to reach Oregon as planned, Starbright laid it on the line for his people.

It kindled interest, which at last grew to enthusiasm. Then came the vote in which the wagon company decided to follow Starbright. Thus he found himself committed, not for days or even weeks, but for months ahead.

Kelly Lang came up to Starbright after the decision, saying, "How soon can we go?"

"Day after tomorrow," said Starbright, then the question rushed out of him. "When they going to get married?"

"I don't know. Rita isn't even speaking to me, any more."

That night Starbright could no longer contain himself. He scowled across the campfire at Wagner and said, "Go ahead. Grin like a monkey. I've got to take these people to Oregon. That's what you wanted, so I got something coming from you. When you going to tie the Lang girl to Redburn?"

Wagner took his pipe from his mouth. He said, "Why didn't you ask me that sooner? I'm not going to."

Starbright was on his feet. "She change her mind?"

"Sit down, Dix. It isn't that good. Redburn asked me to marry them, and I refused."

"Why?" Starbright gasped.

The doctor knocked the dottle from his pipe. Without looking at the mountain man, he said, "I remember a hunting knife I found in the sagebrush. Besides, I'm not sure that I'm still a man of the gospel. I'll practice medicine in Oregon, but I've changed my mind about reporting to the Lee mission." Something dark and deep showed on Wagner's face for the briefest instant. Then he smiled and said, "Don't feel too jubilant, man. They could have the knot tied at the Whitman mission if you get us that far. I think they'll do it. You're driving that girl straight into Redburn's arms."

Yet the relief in Starbright was so great that he could have whooped into the night. Suddenly he was eager for the trail ahead, to prove his ability to take the big company where others said he could not.

CHAPTER TEN

A busy day followed, with the settlers in higher spirits than Starbright had seen them display before. They had known defeat for a time and had brushed it aside. That was tonic for the human spirit, a heady wine.

The trading was completed, the last wagon, the last bit of harness needing it was repaired. In late afternoon, when passing from wagon to wagon, Starbright came at last to the Lang camp where Rita was busy with camp work. Starbright had not yet been able to tell her father that the wedding was off, at least as far as the Whitman mission which was unending weeks ahead.

He grinned wickedly at Rita and said, "Been itching to dance at your wedding. When's it going to be?"

Kelly Lang pulled his body straight and flung a scowl at Starbright.

Rita's head came up, and her eyes narrowed. "So Wagner told you. All right for now, Dix Starbright. It's our hard luck that you made friends with the only preacher in the train. But there'll be other chances — if we live long enough."

The relief that showed in Kelly Lang was

something to see. Starbright looked again at Rita and said, "So Redburn takes the local view of it, does he?"

"He says it's a mad undertaking."

"But he'll consent to come along with us?"

"What else can he do?"

Starbright took up his real business in coming here. To Lang he said, "Figured I ought to warn you. I got my doubts about this big wagon of yours. You've got more draft stock than most, and maybe they can pull it. We'll try. But we might have to drop it."

"Then what?" Lang asked.

"Then you'll have to get along with what you can tie on pack saddles."

"If it comes to that, we'll do it."

Starbright was growing fond of Lang. Though he had hopes of regaining his fortune, probably was thinking of little else, Lang wore his adversity with becoming grace. He was biding his time and meanwhile learning something of the harsher side of frontier life. As was Rita, he thought. She worked as hard and seemed to do as well as any of the other women. He hadn't seen a trace of petulance about it, either.

As far as she knew, her father's gold was gone forever. Poverty would be her permanent lot unless she married Redburn. Starbright doubted that she planned to marry him to escape it. She was taking him partly because he was a man with her background, because he had aroused her pity, and maybe because she knew it would hurt Dix Starbright.

He could not believe that she loved the man very deeply. His memories belied that, for he knew that she could not give to every man what she had one night offered him. That night had been a hard surrender for her and had come from something greater than appetite. Maybe, thought Starbright, the weeks they would now be together would change things for them. They had to put an end to the destructive cycle raging between them. He didn't know how, but he vowed he would do it.

Starbright at last was able to buy the new clothing he had wanted so long.

In late evening, with the wagon party settling for its last night at Fort Hall, he slipped down to the river to make his transformation from a mountain man to a settler. There he bathed and changed, feeling awkward and self-conscious. After buckskins and moccasins, he felt body-bound and found it hard to move about in the boots. He chucked his discarded apparel into the river.

He had turned to start up the bank when he saw the man above him. The figure supported itself by two canes, and Starbright had no idea how long Redburn had been standing there.

"Decided to go civilized?" Redburn asked, then laughed.

"Figured to get rid of my stink. What are you doing here?"

"Waiting to talk to you," Redburn said, and he did wait until Starbright had climbed the bank. Then he said, "I hear you shot off your mouth about me to Kelly Lang. That you accused me of killing his men and stealing the gold."

Starbright reached into a pocket that felt strange to him and pulled out his pipe and tobacco. He loaded the pipe thoughtfully. He said, "In telling Lang, I saved his life. When he told Rita, he was trying to save hers from ruin. Seems to me we both did the right thing. I don't know what woman's notion made her tell you. But I'm glad she did. I been waiting the chance to warn you, myself."

Redburn must have expected a denial or a blustering attitude. Starbright's casual response held the crippled man quiet through a long moment.

"I can't see why you libeled me to Lang instead of Rita, herself," he said. "Unless you knew it would be passed on to her. It did you no good. She doesn't believe you. She's going to marry me at the Whitman mission, if we ever reach the Walla Walla."

"What's libel?" asked Starbright.

"Your outrageous lies!" exploded Redburn.

"I understand the word," said Starbright. "But is the truth libel?"

The starshine and his long illness put the look of age on Tyre Redburn. He really needed his canes for balance and support of his wasted body. His face showed the lines of suffering, probably more mental than physical anguish. The aging of a face, whether through time or other wear, brought out the contents of the mind behind. Redburn's was wasted as he had wasted, was ravished as he had ravished, was wild as he was wild.

Softly he said, "What started you thinking along a line like that?"

"Your big mistake was telling Lang you cleaned up in the fur trade. I know you didn't. And I know you've got sixty thousand in gold in your wagon right now. Gold that Lang and Rita are supposed to believe you started out with. If you'd told him you got that money from your family, I might have accepted it. I wouldn't of known."

"I came by money. I didn't care to tell Lang how. The fur trade made an easy explanation, and I used it."

"You didn't come by money," Starbright snapped, "until the night his three men died by the knife you tried to use on me or by Cob Boze's."

"Can you prove that, Starbright?"

"No. I told Lang what I thought, though, for two reasons. One was to keep him from going back to hunt the men he thought took his gold. That would have suited you fine

141

since your killers didn't get him on the desert. The other reason was to keep him alive if he stayed with the train. Rita doesn't believe what I've said. Just the same, Redburn, if something queer should happen to her father now, she'd be apt to wonder. So you won't try it again. And that's what I aimed to accomplish." In a mockingly polite voice, Starbright added, "Now, shall I help you back to camp?"

Redburn swung up a cane and seemed about to strike him with it. Starbright had wanted to upset his composure and had succeeded.

In a low, shaking voice, Redburn said, "Damn your soul to hell. It isn't finished between us. You think you've ruined me, but I'll get well. I'll beat you every way. And in the end I'll do you worse than you did me."

"You asked for everything you got," Starbright retorted, and he walked off and left the man there.

The wagon company roused cheerfully to the gunshot fired by the guard in first dawn. The chores of breakfast and camp breaking and shaping the loose herd for the trail were quickly accomplished. The bugle rang out and the wagons rolled.

The changed course required them to turn back upon their own tracks for a distance, thereafter following the upper Snake. Two days brought them to the old trapper ford and the tedious, hazardous job of crossing with the wagons.

Here the wagon company experienced its first letdown of spirits. Staring out across the sterile miles of the cutrock desert, it seemed unbelievable that there could be greenery and water beyond. But confidence in Starbright held firmly. The wagons rolled on. It was the severest desert crossing yet made by the train, but it reached the Big Lost without disaster.

Now spirits changed direction and soared again. An enormous sense of triumph surged through the company as it entered the new terrain. It was all that Starbright had promised, as yet it did not disclose what he had also threatened. Lush, wide bottom stood between forested mountains, presenting no great difficulty for the wagons.

Observing too many symptoms of false complacency, Starbright called the company together. "Don't let yourselves be fooled," he said. "Injun danger's always here, even if we don't see any sign. From here till we get back on the main line, we've got to act like a military expedition more than a settler company. Don't forget that a minute."

Thereafter the wagons took punishment and breakdowns became routine. Starbright lost track of time but knew that precious days were slipping by. That in itself carried a menace. Had the company proceeded according to its original plan it could not have reached the settlements before late September or October. It would be exceedingly dangerous for a wagon company to be caught on the high desert east of the Cascade mountains later than that. This detour threatened to make it later, much later. Yet Starbright refused to lend support to impatient haste.

The evening the train reached the Little Wood, Lafferty appeared at the camp of Starbright and Wagner. Lafferty had shaved his cheerful Irish face and donned clean buckskins. His eyes showed a strange mixture of eagerness and reticence.

He looked at Wagner and blurted, "Doc, me and Ruby have got to get married."

Starbright took his pipe from his mouth and grinned across the campfire at the trapper. "Considering she hadn't been kissed proper before Laramie," he drawled, "you done all right, man."

The trapper grinned. "It ain't that kind of got to. It's the kind where we better afore we start a prairie fire. How about it, Doc? You want to bring your book over to the Owen wagon?"

Wagner shook his head. "Out of my line, Lafferty."

Lafferty stared. "Preacher, ain't you?"

"No," said Wagner.

Bewilderment spread over the Irishman's face, that and a heavy disappointment.

Starbright had been watching him and the pretty settler girl called Ruby Owen, making his speculations as to when they would take the jump.

"No," Wagner repeated. "That's out of my line, Lafferty. I'm sorry."

Lafferty started to turn away.

"Wait," said Starbright. "Doc, it's God you're mad at. Not Lafferty and Ruby. They want each other, but they want it to be right. Don't make them do a thing they don't want to do. Make it right for 'em."

Something swirled in Wagner's eyes and for a moment he was silent while he slid his glance over Starbright. Then he said, "When, Lafferty?"

"Right now!" boomed Lafferty.

The word ran through the train that there would be a marriage at the Owen wagon. There was a gleam in Starbrights eyes as he rose to join the throng. He wondered what Rita would think at seeing this other couple married.

The settler Owen was a tall and rangy man and he had a tall and rangy wife. Though sonless, he had two daughters of unusual beauty, and it was the older, the dark-eyed Ruby, who had won Lafferty's heart. Owen had built his campfire high, and the wagon company began to form its big circle about.

When Ralph Wagner stepped into the light, the men pulled off their hats, the women tensing and looking solemn. Lafferty moved up to stand before the doctor with the girl of his choice.

Wagner made it brief, clasping their hands together and covering them with his own. The words he used were quiet, spoken to the principals, and Starbright could not catch what he said. When Wagner tipped his head briefly, the couple followed suit and all around the circle other heads rocked forward.

If Wagner prayed, the words never came across his lips. Yet this beatification was a thing precious to Lafferty and Ruby, and Wagner gave it at least outward form. Then he raised his eyes, smiling, and offered his hand to the trapper. The thing was done.

A nervous titter came from somewhere. Laughter kindled and roared over the crowd. They pressed forward, the men singling out Lafferty to thump his back and congratulate him. The women huddled about the young bride, suddenly wise with their own experience, suddenly sad and yet uplifted. Owen, one of his daughters married off, crossed his arms on his chest and smiled. Starbright saw his wife dab at her eye with a corner of her apron, then begin to serve coffee to the crowd.

"Where you going on your honeymoon?" a man bawled at Lafferty. "We gotta know so we kin shivaree you!"

The trapper took the joke good-naturedly

while the listeners roared. He didn't have his own wagon and at best there was little privacy in a wagon company.

Before going back to his own fire, Starbright walked up to Rita, whose face wore a quiet smile.

He murmured, "Shows what can be done if the man's worth his salt."

She shot him a quick and brittle glance. "A man too bull-headed," she retorted, "can get himself into serious trouble."

Again the wagon train pressed on. It crossed from the Little Wood to the Big Wood river. It seemed that good fortune traveled with it. By now the emigrants had become inured to locking up and roping down and doubling teams on the unending hills. They were used to false starts and painful retracings as they probed their way through the virgin country. Breakdown and repair had become a part of each day's course. If anything, the meeting and overcoming of these obstacles only increased the company's cockiness.

They came at least to Camas Creek and its long, lush valley. Water, grass and game abounded. The going all up the long length of that valley would be easy. Again and again Starbright had to remind his people of the old rule, "The wester, the worser". But they had grown to look upon his steady caution as a chronic pessimism. He knew that they even made private jokes about it. He didn't mind that. If he could not persuade them of what still lay ahead, the trail itself would do it.

The immediate concern in Starbright was suggested by the name the trappers had bestowed on this valley. It was prized by the Indians for the same reasons that the emigrants had sought it. Moreover, they made a substantial use as food of the camas root that grew throughout. If there was to be Indian trouble, this would be the logical place. He kept warning of it, and he doubled the night guard now and increased the herders with the loose stock.

CHAPTER ELEVEN

Yet the trouble came in a way unforeseen by Starbright or any other member of the wagon party. Early on the march, one morning, he grew aware of a blackness on the western horizon that was too sleazy and dirty to be clouds. A little later a band of deer came scudding past, deflecting its course for the train but keeping on due east. Rifles cracked down the length of the train, but the game was too far north.

Starbright, riding with the pilot wagons, had not yet communicated his worry. But within moments after the flight of the deer, he discerned the distant red glow. With the sootiness, it was like a sunrise on a hot morning except that it lay on the wrong horizon. Starbright pulled in a long, slow breath, then quietly told the drivers of the pilot wagon to halt.

"What is that?" a man called to him, worried now. "A fire?"

Starbright only nodded, frowning ahead. For seconds he studied the forward distance. He gave close thought to the terrain more immediately about them, flat except for low swells, and he slid a glance to the parallel lines of hills to right and left. His throat was dry, and there was a sudden slab of tension across his shoulders.

The heavy grass, which had been a lifesaver until now, had in a winking become a deadly menace.

The fire was upwind and growing. Though bearing no visible smoke, the air about now smelled scorched. The fire was new, visibly mounting, and he suspected that it had been set. That meant there were Indians close, perhaps beyond the fire, even all about the train.

Starbright said quietly, "A prairie fire, and it's coming at us. Pass the word down the line. We'll backfire. When we've charred enough grass, we'll pull forward onto it. Maybe the backfire will stop it. If not, we'll have to set in the middle of it while it sweeps around."

"Set? Man, let's get out of here!"

"Drop your voice!" Starbright growled. "These wagons can't outrun it. We can't get them up into the hills. And I'll shoot the first man who tries to start a panic."

He saw that he would have to spread the word himself. Passed wagon to wagon in the usual fashion, it would grow, fear growing with it. He knew what they had to do to survive, and it would be a supreme test of nerve, of courage. He took time to load and light his pipe, not wanting to smoke but to show an unconcern he did not feel.

The forward smoke, perhaps two miles up the valley, tumbled and boiled above intervening objects. Winking in the sooty mantle were the wicked streaks of flame.

"God help us!" a man bawled at a near wagon. "That's a grass fire! It'll get us sure as hell!"

"Simpson, shut up!" Starbright roared.

The man flung him a wild, unseeing stare. He bolted ahead of his oxen and began to belabor them, trying to turn them out of the line and about. Starbright pulled his pistol. He couldn't bring himself to shoot, although the man was seeding the whole line with self-destruction. People were yelling all down the halted wagons now. In a moment they would break.

Starbright drove his horse at the settler with the bullwhack. He bent from the saddle and rapped his gun barrel across the man's head. The man gave out a grunt and fell. His woman shrilly cursed Starbright.

Starbright rode on. His horse had caught the telegraphed apprehension and was skittish. He held it down and rode at an almost leisurely gait, calling to the settler parties as he passed. He saw Lafferty racing up the line of wagons, yelling at others to follow him. The trapper understood the situation, the one narrow way to survive. Wagner was right behind him, with others, steadier men, falling in.

The herd had been trailing behind. When he had passed the last wagon, Starbright lifted his horse to a run. The livestock had milled to an uneasy halt. The mounted herders had congregated on this side. Starbright had to explain over again what he meant to do, backfiring, then pulling the wagons forward onto the burned area.

"But there'll be no holding the herd still," he said. "Drive 'em down there." He pointed to the hills to the south. "Do your best to keep 'em together. But if they explode, let 'em go and save yourselves." The men he addressed were tight with fear. Yet they nodded, and they obeyed. Spreading out, they began to haze the herd south.

Starbright swung his horse and rode the mile to the head of the train. Lafferty and a score of other men had already started backfiring, beginning in the center and working toward either range of hills. They set new fires to the grass at intervals of a hundred feet.

The roaring from the westward fire was like that of a vast waterfall. Smoke now poured into the sky, the flames leaped high. They were generating a concentric draft that Starbright meant to use. The new fires were drawn toward the bigger one. They were fanned and strengthened by its suction. Soon the set fires had come together on a long line that cut the line of the wagons a hundred yards ahead.

Starbright, working and sweating with these cooler men, dared to hope.

But as yet the main fire raged, moving mercilessly toward them. Somewhere down the line of wagons a man's throat gave out a tearing yell. Starbright and the men with him swung about, bathed in sweat and black with soot. Smoke now whipped down about them and the train, and a spot fire had set itself off to the north, well behind the fire line.

Down the line of wagons a span of oxen angled out. A man was pounding them with his whack. The nervous beasts were bucking in their yokes. Starbright roared a protest, every man on the fire line adding voice. But that wagon cut out of line and careened about. Wagons ahead and behind followed suit. Starbright's horse was at a distance from him now. Yet he knew he could not halt what had started.

Panic. Mob panic, senseless and as destructive as the fire that engendered it. The big covered wagons whipped up and pulled out to wheel back on their previous line of march. Behind them there was falsely reassuring ground. Walkers scrambled aboard or attempted to run, the whole train thrown suddenly into turmoil.

Starbright raced for his horse although aware of his impotence. The goaded oxen ran at a gallop. Wagons lurched on the rough ground. Then the loose herd, still moving

153

across the valley, caught the contagion and blew apart. Horses, oxen, cattle — they swung and bolted down the valley, the way the wagons were headed, the way the deer had gone.

Starbright turned from his horse and walked back to the fire line. The men who had helped him there still stood firm, doubling their efforts now that everything depended upon their success. There was a wide band of char now, still smoking and glowing. Thermals generated by the original blaze sucked the new ones toward it, giving them impetus and something of its own ferocity.

Sweat-soaked and all but collapsing from exhaustion, Starbright at last saw the two fires come together like giant beasts from the nether world joining in combat. But the prairie fire was stabilized except for its extreme ends. The men raced toward these wings to beat them down.

Wagner appeared beside Starbright, staring back toward the scampering wagons.

"God help them!" he breathed.

"Goddamn them!" growled Starbright.

He could see that half a dozen wagons had overturned, the downed oxen struggling and kicking helplessly. People ran on afoot, abandoned, unthinking, powered by the roaring instinct of self-survival. Beyond those few grim sights, all was lost in dust, a mantle as vast and now more dangerous than the smoke on the other horizon.

Lafferty came up, gagging for breath. No wagon had escaped the panic. Such drivers as had kept their heads had been unable to restrain their beasts. Lafferty's bride was lost in the eastward dust.

"If they'd only waited!" he panted. "We got her licked!"

Westward the smoke boiled into the sky, flames still tonguing through it awesomely. A choking mixture of smoke, heat and gas lay over the whole prairie. But the fire, Starbright dared to hope, had been halted. They had burned nearly a mile of its downwind course. Now they bent their efforts to beating out the spot fires.

Then at last sanity began to return to the scene. The dust gradually cleared away, disclosing for as far as the eye could see the shapes of halted wagons, widely scattered. At least a dozen had overturned, and Starbright knew that on the ground lay trampled bodies.

Then he called Lafferty aside and said, "We got to pull them together fast, man. Snakes set this. Next thing we got to expect is an attack from them."

"I'm scared of it," Lafferty admitted.

Starbright rode the scene of devastation, turned sick by what he found. Of the dozen overturned wagons, half were wrecked beyond repair. But there was worse. Some of the occupants had been thrown out to be overrun by vehicles and maddened cattle coming on behind. Others, racing afoot in the blinding dust, had been run down.

Swearing like a madman, his tongue cutting like a blacksnake whip, Starbright ordered the survivors to pull themselves together and form a wagon circle. Lame cattle and damaged wagons again moved, the drivers spent, remorseful, bewildered. At last a sorry looking wagon camp was built on the bank of the creek, in the valley that had been so beautiful, in the security that had been false.

With a mirthless grin, Lafferty spoke to Starbright. "You won't get a man to admit he up and run. The oxen'll be blamed for it all. And you, Starbright."

He had judged the situation shrewdly. When Starbright had secured the company as best he could against the Indian attack he now feared, he ordered the dead and hurt brought in. There were only three men among the destroyed but five women and four children. A score of others had been hurt, a woman had given birth on the trampled ground.

The company began to make its accusations back and forth, accusing each other and admitting no fault, no man succeeding in persuading even himself. Therefore a target was needed, and that target lay in Starbright. He could feel the resentment building, in the way they looked at him and responded to his savage orders.

At last he called them together. He said, "What's done is done, and we got to think of what to do next. The Snakes started the fire. It could be they only wanted to scatter the herd and latch onto some stock. And put a few wagons and whites out of business. They succeeded well, and God pity your souls for helping. Now they may be encouraged to attack us. We've got to expect it and be ready."

"God in heaven!" a settler bawled. "Ain't we had enough?"

"Ask Him, not me," Starbright retorted. "To my count, half a dozen wagons will never roll out of this valley. We'll use them to patch up the ones we can. We'll try and round up our stock. We'll make packsaddles and take on what we can from the dropped wagons. That's the best we can do."

"Damn your fool head, Starbright!" the same speaker persisted. "We agreed to come this way, but we never really knew what we were getting into. You did. Sure you warned us. But you had no damned business coaxing us."

"You never said truer," Starbright agreed.

"You got us in a hell of a fix!" the man went on in mounting fury. "God knows how long we'll be gettin' ready to go again! We're apt to hit worse than this!"

"Wait a minute," Kelly Lang cut in. "My

157

wagon will have to be dropped. I've got two smashed wheels. But it's my own damned fault. I had a part in the parade we put on. I got the hell scared out of me and just did what every other damned fool was doing. And that's where the damage was done. Even an idiot like myself can see we'd have been all right if we'd obeyed orders."

The company needed a scapegoat to which it could shift its terrible weight of guilt. But it also needed a leader, and Starbright was the only one who had been through the country ahead. The threatened revolt subsided.

Yet Starbright's own nerves were in rebellion. For the moment, he hated the people about him. But he had proposed this route, he had betrayed his enthusiasms for attempting it. Therefore it was his responsibility to take them on.

The valley on west of them was now only a vast sea of feebly smoking black char. Wagner ordered the dead buried at once in a mass grave. That was done in the night so that the Indians could not observe and later desecrate it. When the train moved again, Starbright would have the wagons run over the grave to obliterate it.

Before, during, and after that grim ceremony, the camp awaited the feared attack from the Snakes. But daylight came without its having happened. Now Starbright gave thought to rounding up the scattered animals, which included everything that had not been hooked to a wagon and the few horses that had had riders. Starbright told Lafferty to pick as many men as could be mounted and go after the stock. Neither of them had hopes of recovering more than a small part. They could dispense with the milch cows and horses, if necessary, but they needed every extra draft steer they could bring back.

The train was pinned down on Camas Creek for nearly two weeks, precious weeks that cut a somber piece off the good weather remaining for the crossing to be concluded. Men scoured the hills for stock. They repaired wagons and made pack saddles. But the hurt ones were allowed to recover somewhat in comparative comfort.

Then came a morning when the party broke camp to move west once more. It was a discouraged, all but beaten group, leaving dead behind in a mass and obliterated grave, leaving the picked skeletons of wagons and many other possessions and two-thirds of the livestock. And the way ahead grew rougher, more rugged each day.

A few hours of travel took them to the place where the fire had been set. Investigating with Lafferty, Starbright confirmed his opinion that it was Indian work. A little westward was the place where an Indian village had been for a considerable time, then had been dismantled and removed.

The Sawtooths now crowded down upon them, with a spur of the same mountains hooking in from the south. Where the two formations came together, a summit had to be crossed. Starbright doubted that either the people or the animals were capable of doing it, to say nothing of the wagons. But once over there would be no barrier between them and the Oregon Trail. That was the purpose in Starbright. He drove himself and people toward the mountains and into the mountains. Had it been flat, the distance would have required a day's march. As it was there came a week of struggle.

When they came down at last upon a creek, with the mountains close behind, they were short four more wagons. Much of the livestock was sick, sorefooted, played out. There was nothing to do but rest again with each day precious. Starbright found a fair campsite on the creek and ordered a layover.

It was a popular decision, though taking time they could ill afford. Despair was eating into the company, the dangerous kind of chronic exhaustion that could wear away the human will.

Starbright's own camp, still shared with Ralph Wagner, was out under the wheeling stars. The stock, a shrunken, sorry-looking bunch now, was downstream. There were ten packing parties with the train now, families deprived of their wagons. Each had attached itself to a going wagon for traveling and to camp. The Langs had thrown in with the Owens, the family into which Lafferty had married. There was satisfaction in that for Starbright. If Rita had wanted to attach to Tyre Redburn's wagon, Kelly Lang had stopped that cold.

Lafferty came to Starbright's camp in the late evening. He said, "This company could stand some fresh meat. It's around here. If enough of us went out tomorrow, we might get enough to knock the edges off our appetites."

Starbright was interested, although he frowned slightly. Lafferty's indirectness showed that he understood the objection to such a venture. If there were Indians spying on the train, and the chances were good that there were, the scattering of any great number of the men might be an invitation for them to attack. To hunt here safely, the hunters would have to deploy in squads, since a lone man would stand to lose his hair.

"He's right," Wagner said to Starbright. "The company's worn to the bone and gristle. The weather's getting colder. When the rains come, we're ripe for an epidemic. It's worried me. We need more red meat. We ought to do more hunting."

"All right," Starbright agreed. "You can take out a party, Lafferty. I don't feel I ought to leave the train."

"There's Redburn," Lafferty said promptly. "He's throwed away his canes. He's put on weight. Looks to me he's as good as ever."

Starbright knew that through the last days Tyre Redburn had been walking with his wagon and without his canes. Since Fort Hall he had driven himself, fighting for strength, for full recovery, and little by little Starbright had seen the steel will of the man establish its supremacy over his tortured flesh.

"How about that, Doc?" Starbright asked.

"If he's not as good as ever, he probably will be. I think the blood clot's dissolved. Or else he's forced his system to make alternate adjustments. He told me that God and the devil combined couldn't keep him from becoming stronger than you, Starbright. You know why."

"Sure," Lafferty put in. "Figures he's the one going to marry Rita Lang."

"Tell him he can take out a party, too, if he wants," Starbright said to Lafferty and watched the man walk off.

Lafferty left in the following daylight with a squad of eight hunters. Starbright was surprised to hear that Redburn had declined to lead a second party, claiming that he was not equal to it. For a moment Starbright considered leaving the train to go, himself. Redburn would be in camp in case there were signs of Indian trouble. Yet somehow Starbright distrusted that possibility. The past had given him grim proof that Redburn would act first in self-interest, thereafter in the interest of others only if it suited him.

The day passed in quiet industry. The continual wagon repairs went on, the continual treating of stock. Again the women seized the chance to wash clothing and to cook for the journey ahead. Again the children had a new vicinity to explore and went noisily and energetically at it.

The hunters were back at noon, the horses they had ridden forth loaded with the carcasses of the mule deer typical of sageland plateau and the lower timber. That would have been a lot of meat for a smaller train. It was only a dab with this one. But Lafferty shook his head when Starbright asked if they were going out again.

Calling Starbright aside, he said, "I seen Injun sign, man. Said nothing to the others but I knew we were watched. I spent all morning with my heart in my nose. By and by I'll make a little circle and see what's got its eye on this camp."

Starbright felt his cheeks stiffen. He nodded. He knew from his own experience with tribes farther east that no wagon company ever passed through without being watched steadily, and rarely with friendly eyes. Whether an attack came depended entirely on the circumstances, the size of the train or the size of the tribe available for fighting. Though large, this train had been in the hinterland for weeks. There had been ample time for recruitment among the redskins, time for councils and war dances. Now the train was pulling down on Snake River again. It soon would be out of striking distance. An attack would come soon if it was to come at all.

Lafferty slipped away to scout and was back within two hours. He tipped Starbright a guarded nod as he came into the camp. He got a towel and soap and went down to the creek. Presently Starbright quietly followed him.

"Make your plans," Lafferty drawled. "You're going to catch it." He pointed east. "They're back there. No squaws, no kids, and the bucks stripped down for fighting. I'd say a hundred. And a couple hundred ponies. Means they want prisoners and plunder. Been recruiting going on. They been building up to our size."

Starbright felt a touch of cold dread. But his mind accepted and quickened at once to the problem. Superstition kept most Indians from fighting at night if they could help it. They rarely did so voluntarily. The Snakes had been encamped when Lafferty spied upon them, which seemed to indicate that they had no aggressive plans for that day.

Therefore two possibilities presented themselves to Starbright. The wagons could roll at once and hope to run away from the trouble. Or they could stay put and meet what came.

Starbright decided to stick to course, prepared for an attack. He had the loose stock brought in and penned in the wagon circle. Afterward he drew some of the men aside. This train had never stood off an Indian assault. He told them what to expect, what to do if one came. The Snakes, he explained, might come in mounted and apply their circling siege. Again they might attempt to sneak in, crawling through the sage, in hope of achieving surprise.

The faces of the listeners showed a deepened gravity. But the men took the shock of it and made their individual adjustments. Because of the stock and its dust, a community fire was built outside the ring, near the creek. The women busied themselves with their cooking. Youngsters dragged up fuel.

Lafferty had slipped away, moving east again to watch. Starbright watched the sun slide down the sky, hoping against hope that it would touch the far mountains and slide away with peace still upon this great empty world.

Yet around five o'clock, with two or three hours of daylight left, Starbright saw Lafferty driving in upon the camp, using his cap to whip his horse. He came openly and he came fast. Starbright felt a moment of despair, then energy pumped into him.

Lafferty bawled out as he came on, secrecy now of no worth. "Injuns! Get set!"

Men ran for their stations, rushing wives and children into their wagons, a few women making shrill rollcalls of their young. The food, almost ready to be eaten, was left at the fire. Lafferty slid his horse to a halt by Starbright.

He said, "Small party coming first. Wearin' blankets so we can't see they're armed. The big party's waiting for 'em to throw us off guard. They don't know they've been seen and tallied."

"We won't let any of them come close," Starbright decided.

It seemed a long while before he saw anything appear in the east to excite him. The late hour of the day told him he had to defend the train, not from a full and wearing assault, but a swift, fierce raid that would sweep in, raise pandemonium, and be gone again with stock, scalps, women. There was no defense against it except steady gunfire.

Then at last Starbright discerned a dust to the easy and then the shapes of oncoming ponies. They came slowly, the riders bareback, slack and lazy. They seemed in no hurry. There were half a dozen of them.

When they were within earshot, Starbright

166

fired a pistol into the air. He saw them halt, jump from their ponies and scatter into the sage. But the shot was mainly a signal to the guards Starbright had put out. They began their retreat toward the wagons. Thereafter nothing but the sagebrush was in view. More time passed in which Starbright dared to hope that a reprieve would somehow come. He kept watching the sky with its softening light. Then he heard Lafferty's explosive curse and slid his glance out the way the trapper pointed.

Ponies boiled out of the notch in the hills and came on openly. It was the whole war party, informed that a surprise on the train was impossible. Within moments the white people could hear their shrieks above the rumbling of the ponies' hoofs. A main body clung together, sections breaking off on either side, fanning out. Many of them carried rifles. Others had only bows and arrows. They all had scalping knives and belt hatchets.

At last Starbright and Lafferty stepped back into the protection of the wagons. The train guards were in. Then, in a single explosion of fury, the entire train made challenge.

The Snakes drove straight on the train. They meant to overwhelm it and while knowing this the settlers were cool. They faced death. They had to fight it. Starbright, using a pistol, knocked a buck off a horse. He dropped the pony of another. Indian balls and arrows thunked into the wagon as the two wings of the assault drove past. Now women broke and began to scream, the children following suit. From here and there came the hoarse shout of a wounded man.

Dust boiled up so that Starbright could see only a few yards about him. When something appeared out of it he shot and calmly reloaded. Now the Snakes had slid off their ponies; they were rushing the train afoot. A hundred warriors, Lafferty had estimated, but now there seemed a thousand.

They swept across the wagon circle, and the one fight became a multitude of individual struggles. When men fell women seized up their rifles. Others went down under knives and hatchets. Scalps began to lift. Starbright saw a young girl dragged out into the sage, but at that instant something hurtled itself at him through the dust, hitting his back.

Starbright bent forward, throwing the figure across his shoulders and over onto the tramped ground. He leaped forward and used his pistol butt to smash a painted, sweaty head. The fight swirled on, with no pause, with no quarter. Then, their objective accomplished, the Snakes pulled off. Somewhere they had opened the wagon circle and run out stock. They had used brands from the big cook fire to ignite several wagons and the blazing showed itself to Starbright through the thick dust. The Snakes were satisfied. They went up to their ponies again, and they went into retreat.

Thereafter there were the blazing wagons to think of. They were uncoupled hastily and pulled out of line, while bucket brigades tried to form out of the chaos to bring water from the creek. Ralph Wagner rushed from still figure to still figure. Everywhere they called for him and for Starbright. Some saw their dead on the ground and were less terrified than those who could not find their kin and friends.

The dust cleared away, though out in the sage wagons still blazed fiercely, reducing themselves to wreckage, their steel red hot. Yet a degree of order, however horrible, returned to the camp. Starbright saw Tyre Redburn standing by a burned wagon. He stood motionless, a look of twisted anguish on his face. Redburn was not contemplating the mutilated body of a loved one. There had been gold in his wagon, and now his wagon had burned without his having been able to save the gold.

Kelly Lang came lurching toward Starbright. He said, "Have you seen Rita? I can't find her."

Oh God! Starbright thought then.

CHAPTER TWELVE

Starbright swung back to Redburn.

"Hear that, man? The Injuns finally got her."

Redburn's eyes were glinting pits in the faint light still coming from his destroyed wagon.

He gasped, "You think it was Walking Crow?"

"What does it matter? You've still got the gold. It never burned. When it cools you'll have you a lump that's worth a fortune. And there's lots of women."

By dawn the men, children, and older women of the company had been accounted for among the living, the hurt, the dead. In the first light, searchers beating around the camp found younger women, a few barely matured, supine in the sage, ravished, scalped, stabbed. Sight after grisly sight they were come upon, the aftermath of orgy encircling the aftermath of struggle. The grim accounting was completed with one exception. Nothing was found of Rita Lang, nothing was remembered to throw light upon her fate. She was missing, and that eloquent fact drove Starbright incessantly on.

He found Lafferty and said, "Take over. Get going as soon as you can. Get to Fort Boise before you stop to lick your wounds."

"What you going to do?" Lafferty asked narrowly.

"I'm going after her."

The trapper made a sweep of the arm that included all the hills. "You'll never find her. Or if you do, you won't want what you find."

"I'll find her," said Starbright. "If I go a thousand miles and a thousand days, I'll find her. Or what's left. One thing or the other, I'll do it."

"That you will," agreed Lafferty.

Starbright's saddle horse had escaped the plundering. He cinched on the saddle and led the animal to his camp. Wagner was there, stretched exhausted on the earth. He lifted his head to stare up at Starbright, who began to fill his saddlebags from their provisions, to add an extra can of gun powder, a box of caps, and a pouch of balls. Wagner, understanding, shook his head and watched through blood-streaked eyes. He made a bitter, pushing motion of the hand at all the country about them.

He said, "You were cut out for it, Starbright. I wasn't."

"Take it easy, Doc. It's worse for you. You already lost a girl like those we brought in this morning."

"Haven't you?"

"God knows."

"And cares?" asked Wagner.

"Doc," said Starbright, "you're trying to look through a mountain. Don't do it. It's there to be climbed and when you come to the top, maybe you'll know about that."

Wagner rose and held forth his hand, saying, "Take care."

"Tell Lang I'm going after her," Starbright said and rose to the saddle.

A feeble hope guttered in him. To his fevered, darting mind the situation spelled out certain facts. The Snakes had used their female captives close to the camp then discarded them. That meant that they had not wanted to be encumbered by prisoners in their flight from the white men's wrath. Yet Rita was a prize specimen of a woman to any man. She would make an enviable slave and toy for some village chief. Any buck holding her captive could trade her for many horses or several squaws. Since she alone had been taken away, there was a chance that she would not be killed or even abused until she had reached some remote village.

This it was that pulled Starbright on. The sign he followed was plain. The Snakes had retreated along the old Indian trail the wagons had followed. Midday found Starbright crossing a land of rolling sage, broken now and then by a declivity or some small stream. The trail wound down and up, back and forth through the wasteland, the sign remaining plain. The Snakes had come together and were now moving in a single body. He judged that they were heading back to the valley of the Camas where they had worked their first vengeance against the company.

He kept on doggedly, warily, behind them. Two hours passed, then he came upon a problem. The Snakes had halted, apparently to powwow, and then the band had broken up. A few had gone on along the trail, larger contingents had turned north away from it. He dismounted and walked about. He would as leave have only a small party to contend with when he caught up, but which of the diverging parties had Rita with it? He sifted the situation and made a gambler's decision.

Lust was satisfied, and the Snakes were breaking up to lose themselves in the hills. Yet the easiest route for a warrior with a captive would be the trail. Starbright remounted and rode on. He had danger on either hand now, as well as ahead, yet he brushed the fact aside and dogged on.

It was now a forbidding land of sage, volcanic rock and an awesome vacantness. Now and then he halted to dismount and rest his horse. Once he ate cold from the saddlebags and smoked his pipe. Weariness from a day's march, a fight, a night of disaster, then this day's trailing accumulated in his body. It ached, yet was a detached feeling which he disowned and ignored.

Then he came upon droppings so fresh they were still moist and was wholly energized. The trail was scuffed, wheel-tracked and hoof-marked, telling him little except for unmistakably fresh sign. Now he knew that his quarry could not be far ahead. As near as he could estimate, he was following half a dozen Indian ponies with no assurance that one was ridden by Rita.

Timber country lay ahead, and the day was now dying. The Indians would make camp, for they did not like the supernatural beings they believed to prowl the world in the dark. He slowed his pace then, patient, always patient. He was soon in the timber and its pools of shadow and its coolness.

He watched his horse carefully and at last bent swiftly forward to stop its urge to whicker. That meant it had caught a fresh scent left in the air by its own kind. Now Starbright pulled off the trail and swung down. He did not want to pause a moment longer than necessary. Encamped with Rita, the Snakes might change their plan for her as their spent appetites began to return. If she was with this party — always there was that doubt to nag him.

He let an hour pass then started on afoot. He had gone about a mile when he discerned the winking light of a small campfire ahead in the woods. He was up against men even more completely adapted to the wilderness than he was himself. Yet he was again a mountain man, on his own in an unfriendly and unknown land. He checked his pistols and shoved them back. He moved forward, skulking from tree to tree. He paused to listen through long moments. He sniffed the air like a wary animal.

Then at last he was in above the fire and could see the figures about it. He counted five, and his heart sank. All were the glistening, naked bodies of Indians. He could not discern the shape of a woman. He pulled up his guns, one in either hand. He sucked in a slow and silent breath. Then he went in upon the Indian camp, emptying each gun.

The figures leaped up together except for two that slowly bent over and went limp on the ground. The other three, howling fearfully, bounded for the far darkness. By then Starbright was at the camp, and there he saw Rita. She lay on the ground, face down, and was bound with buckskin thongs. She raised her head and stared toward him, and her face showed only terror.

"It's Starbright," he called and came to her, emerging into the firelight.

Arms lay about, two rifles, bows and arrows. He decided that one of the escaped bucks had paused to seize a weapon. He didn't stop moving. Seizing Rita, he dragged her back into the darkness. Even then he only bent and lifted her, then went pounding back along his own course.

When he had gone a hundred yards, he stopped and put her down. His hunting knife quickly cut her bonds. In a torn and broken way, she kept saying, "Starbright . . . Starbright . . ."

"You all right?"

"Yes."

"They didn't — ?" He couldn't bring himself to complete the question.

"They didn't. Not yet. But they were quarreling over who — who'd be first."

She had been bound and motionless too long to move on her own just then. Starbright swung her across his shoulder and went on. He came at last to the place where he thought he had left his horse. It was not there or, as he began to realize, he had not come to the right place. He cursed silently, swinging right and left in puzzlement. He could hear other horses running in the distance. The surviving bucks had reached their picketed ponies. They would return to the camp and arm themselves. In a moment they would be giving hot pursuit.

His horse had not strayed. He had misjudged direction in his flight with Rita. Now he had to lose time while he found the place where he had left the animal. He could hear a wild calling in the distance as the Snakes got organized to pursue. By now they knew that he had taken Rita; they were beating the brush closer to the camp. Revenge on both of them would now be swift and merciless. Starbright reluctantly gave up hope of finding his horse in time. He plunged on into the deeper timber with Rita.

He was all but exhausted, long later, when she said, "You can't keep this up. Let me down. I'll walk somehow."

He stopped then and let her slide down his body to the ground. The Snakes' outcry had all but faded out behind them. Rita leaned on him to steady herself and they went on.

Starbright kept it up for three hours before stopping. He said, "I think we got away from them. Now we've got to rest. There's no hope of getting my horse. That means we've got no grub. It must be thirty miles to where our wagons were camped. We'll get there to find 'em gone and have to hoof it to Fort Boise."

He knew she was exhausted, incapable of going farther. They were in a ravine, and Starbright cut boughs with his knife, working until he had a pile of them. He found a place under a low-skirted young pine and spread out the boughs. In a voice ragged with tiredness, he said, "Burrow down in 'em, Rita. We'll have to hug each other to keep warm."

She obeyed him, and when he had

stretched himself beside her he pulled more boughs over them against the crisp mountain air. Her spent body pressed the length of his side, and she let an arm fall across him. He could feel her breath warm and hurried on his neck, the greater pressure of a breast, the touch of her thigh. They were shut off from the Snakes, the world, in a green cocoon.

"Dad?" she whispered.

"All right," Starbright told her. "But it was bad. Don't talk of it now."

She did not ask about Tyre Redburn.

He wasn't aware of falling asleep, but suddenly opened his eyes to see daylight sifting in through the greenery. He turned his head to see that neither he nor Rita had stirred in the hours in which they had slept. The boughs had trapped the heat of their flesh and she still slept, molded against him, her arm still across him. For a long moment he watched her reposed face. At last he pressed his lips to her cheek, and this awakened her.

"Got a long way to go on empty bellies," he said. "Best get at it."

"I think we'll make it."

All through a long day, Starbright led the way, eschewing the main trail but skirting it, not knowing at what moment they might stumble upon one of the other Indian parties. In late afternoon he grew fearful of Rita's ability to keep on. She made no complaint but her unsteady steps, her drained face were eloquent of exhaustion.

Starbright wanted to keep going. He had carried out his purpose earlier than he had dared to hope. Now there was a chance that they could reach the wagons before they had broken camp. He doubted that Rita could keep going, but when he spoke to her of his hopes, she said, "We'll make it, Starbright."

Then, somewhere deep in the night, they topped a rise to see campfires far below them. "They're still there!" shouted Starbright.

The wagon train had found many tasks to keep it there. Again a mass grave had been prepared and filled. There were severely wounded ones to be transported as far as Fort Boise. The company was too beaten to be hurried or greatly worried, any more.

When Starbright came into the big camp with Rita, it was bedded down for the night save for the guard and a few of the sleepless. Among these were Kelly Lang, who, discerning the new arrivals, let out a great shout. Wagner was up, and so were Lafferty and Redburn. The change, the deliverance, pumped new energy through them all. For the moment the tragedy seemed offset by victory.

Kelly Lang clenched his fists and shoved them at the sky and cried, "Thank God! Thank God!" Wagner's face wore a smile, while Lafferty grinned from ear to ear.

But Tyre Redburn stared at Starbright from a wooden face. He slid his glance to Rita. He said nothing. Starbright felt his hackles rise at the man's odd preoccupation. In that instant the old friction struck a spark and sprung into flame.

In a drawling voice, Starbright said, "I got your girl for you, Redburn. I spent a night with her in the hills."

There was a low cry from Rita, then she fled. Kelly Lang shot Starbright an angry look and followed.

"Won't you ever learn, Starbright?" asked Wagner. "Will you ever get onto yourself?"

Lafferty walked off with Starbright and Wagner. When they were out of earshot of Redburn, Lafferty halted.

He said, "Starbright, you done a fine thing, and I hand it to you. But you ought to have your goddamn teeth kicked down your throat. You ought to have your tongue yanked out. And I'd like to do it."

"Go ahead," said Starbright. "I wasn't even thinking of her and Lang. It was Redburn and the way he looked at me. His eyes like rattler's. Hating me for something he should of done and could have. It didn't set right on me. It pulled that out."

"Go apologize to them, Dix," said Wagner. His voice was quiet but carried something that made Starbright glance at him sharply.

"All right."

When he reached the Owen camp, Rita was already rolled up in blankets. So were the Owens and Lafferty's wife. Lang was still by the fire, sitting there, frowning at the new arrival.

"Lang," said Starbright, "I went crazy. I'm sorry. There wasn't a thing in what I said. That was for Redburn. I had to rowel him."

For a moment Lang was quiet. Then he shrugged, saying, "We're grateful to you, Starbright. Deeply grateful. We'll forget it. We've got to. We all need each other too much."

Rita stirred. She was awake, but she said nothing. Turning about, Starbright walked away.

The dawn and promise of renewed marching lifted the company from its depression. Most of the newly scattered livestock had been brought back the day before. Eight more wagons were being dropped, and the oxen thus released were put in the pool of reserve draft power. The remaining wagons had been put in shape to travel.

Redburn and his man Boze had put in the preceding day building a crude packsaddle. This morning they put it on one of their steers. The patient animal accepted the blanket and saddle. Redburn had saved nothing from his burned wagon but a steel chest that now was scorched and discolored. Starbright observed that he and Boze were

181

trying to lash the chest to the saddle.

"Too damned heavy," said Boze. "Must weigh three hundred. We'll have to put it on one side and lash something just as heavy on the other. That's going to poop the critter."

"We'll lash it on," said Redburn.

Lang, standing near, flung Starbright a quick and pregnant glance. Starbright walked over to the sweating pair, Lang following.

"That chest got pretty hot," said Lang. "Probably it holds nothing but bullion now. Tried to open it?"

"Stuck shut," Redburn said grudgingly.

Starbright, enjoying the discomfort in the man, said, "Better turn your precious gold over to somebody with a wagon. Or don't you trust anybody?"

"I'll do the worrying," Redburn snapped.

Kelly Lang, sliding his gaze from the chest to Redburn, said, "Nice of you to do that for me, Tyre."

Redburn's shoulders lifted, his eyes narrowing. "I know you've swallowed Starbright's lies, Lang. But you'd better watch your remarks."

"Not lies."

"He lied," Redburn said harshly. "This is my gold. I'll keep it."

"Mine," said Lang. "And I'll get it back."

The wagons toiled in to Fort Boise under a leaden sky. Lafferty let a worried gaze probe the overhead and said, "Making bag, Dix. We don't get the sun on us much from here on. Rain means mud, and mud means half the travel each day. Twice the wear on the cattle. There's mountains ahead. Big ones. There's rivers. Mean ones. Pretty soon, when it ain't rainin', there'll be frost. Snow. God, it's a long ways to Oregon."

CHAPTER THIRTEEN

The wagons stayed two days at the fort.
Wagner had the more seriously wounded carried within to be left behind either to die or
to recover, four men and a woman too far
gone to travel farther. It was a hard decision
for him, Starbright knew, and he was torn
between his desire to remain and care for
them and his greater responsibility to go on
with those who perhaps needed him more.
But the fort people were experienced in
rough medicine, surgery and nursing. The
abandoned were not being left to their fate.

Redburn bought a two-wheel cart left by
an earlier train, a span of oxen and a new
camp outfit. Starbright was able to obtain a
good riding horse and saddle, to obtain
powder, caps and balls for his pistols.

The rain continued for three days, on the
last of which the harried train crept out
again, now driving on the dangerous Snake
River crossing. Starbright pushed it hard,
fearing that the rain would have brought up
the river to pin them down perhaps for
weeks. Then the rain stopped, the sky
cleared, and on the fourth day they came to
the crossing.

The Snake was a broad and wicked stream, seen at first from the top of high palisades. The descent to its level was made through the canyon of a sidestream, a hard, rough drop that many a wagon had taken before them. At the bottom, and ahead of his people, Starbright sat his horse for a long while. The river was wide, a great deal of it seemed to be swimming water.

All the wagon traffic past this point was moving west. Raft after raft had been built and used and abandoned on the far shore to float away. Now Starbright and his people faced the same slow, wearing task of building anew, the timbers snaked in from distant timber and lashed together here. Thereafter would come the monotonous, endless crossing, wagon by wagon, and the swimming of the loose herd, the reassembling and resumption of the grueling trail. Lafferty had been right. It was a long, hard piece to Oregon.

It took a week to make the crossing. Seven days of driving work from dawn to dusk. Every wagon was crossed safely, a few steers were lost in the swimming. The train wound up the tough canyons of Burnt River toward the Blue Mountains. Despair began again to ride with it. The Blues were as bad as any mountains behind. Thereafter was more desert, the long reach of the Columbia. Finally, irony of ironies, came the last barrier, the all but insuperable Cascades on the very edge of the Willamette Valley, the heart-break point of the trail.

They fought through the Burnt canyon and came out again in valley land. They reached the Powder and went numbly on toward the Blues. There was a drive in the company now that aroused dread in Starbright. They would reach the Columbia at Fort Walla Walla.

Before then would come the Whitman mission on the Walla Walla River. There, Starbright had forgotten, would come Rita's next chance to marry Redburn. It preyed on his mind constantly. He wondered if she would do it. He feared that she would. She had renewed her loathing of him after their return from the escape from the Snakes.

Then in the middle of a cold, gray afternoon they topped a high, dividing ridge to come down into a valley the trappers had named the Grande Ronde — Great Circle. It was a beautiful basin covered by rich grass, hemmed in by high, heavily timbered mountains.

To Wagner, Starbright said: "We ought to rest again before we tackle the Blues. They'll be bad, all the way to the Walla Walla Valley. This is once when the people won't want to do it. They see the Columbia in their minds. But we ought to stop and feed up the stock, if nothing else. Hard pull ahead."

"And fill up the people," Wagner agreed.

"Great Scott, how we need red meat. I dream of it. I could eat it raw. And green stuff. A woman told me she thought she'd trade her virtue for a mess of turnip greens."

"We'll camp," Starbright decided. "Elk around here. We'll eat red meat. We'll let the stock have the greens."

They pulled on to the river that day. When Starbright passed the word to set up for a two-day camp it was at first received grumpily. Yet, once halted, they began to relax and dismiss their drives. By morning it was an all but happy camp.

Lafferty went out early with horses and a large hunting party. Once more there were plans for a feast, a dance — the festivities that had been so tragically disrupted beyond Fort Boise. But this was the country of the Nez Perces, a friendlier people.

A woman sought Wagner, saying, "Doctor, I think it would be nice to have church while we're here. We did till we came to the pass. I've missed that comfort."

Starbright, listening, put a veiled glance on Wagner. The woman had lost her husband to the Snakes. She had seven children, the oldest a thin, overworked boy of thirteen.

Wagner took his pipe from his lips to say, "No reason why we couldn't have it."

"You'll lead us?"

"I've taken care of the sick and hurt," said

Wagner. He started to say more, but his voice trailed off.

"We need more than that," the woman said. "You've got what we need."

"Ah, no," said Wagner. "I haven't got it. I never had it, though I thought I did."

"You've turned bitter."

"Haven't you?"

"No," the woman said and walked away.

Starbright busied himself going from party to party within the big company. No one now needed urging to look after his wagon and stock during a layover. He went on to where some of the young bucks had dragged up logs for a big bonfire. Some girls were there, sitting on the logs and talking and dreaming their secret dreams.

Starbright found himself at the Owen wagon. Lang and Owen had gone out with the hunters. The women were busy at camp work, Rita helping them. Starbright smiled at Rita, who returned it with a nod and the merest frown.

He said, "Want to help me build another fish trap?"

She said, "Why, maybe I do."

"Come along then," he said.

They moved off down the river but not far. When they came to a riffle and its ensuing pool, Starbright got out his hunting knife and began to hack sprouts. He showed Rita how to build the trap, sticking in the slender poles and weaving a fence. When they were done, they sat on the bank above the trap.

"You haven't forgiven me," he said.

She looked at him quickly, saying, "What's forgiveness?"

"Canceling it off. Marking it paid."

"It's not paid. It can't be canceled. You pull too hard, Starbright. Then you turn around and hit too hard. I'd never trust you again."

"You got a punch, yourself," he said.

"I guess." She smiled ruefully. "I'm made like you are. When somebody hits me, I've got to hit him. If he doesn't like me, I don't like him. That's weak. It's terrible. But a fact."

"Work the same way when somebody loves you?"

"You don't. Love's got tenderness in it. You want my body the way a stag wants a doe, a bull a cow, a stud a mare. I've got two legs, Starbright, not four. I've got affection and not just lust."

His cheeks stung, and he frowned. "Redburn's got tenderness?"

"Yes."

"Glad I don't, then," Starbright drawled.

She flung him a quick glance. "He took a girl away from you once before, didn't he? I've been grilling Lafferty. He won't say much. But from what he does and from what I heard the night you stopped the train out

189

of Laramie, I think he beat your time with a squaw. You can't stand the thought of it again. So you've lied about him to my father. You make your dark hints to me. It gets you nowhere, Dix Starbright. I understand you. I loathe you."

"Still going to marry Redburn?"

"At the first chance."

"That'll be the Whitman mission, across the hills."

"I know. I'm looking forward to it."

Rita rose lightly and walked away, not even looking at their fish trap.

Lafferty's hunters had luck. They came in packing three elk, animals as large as steers. By nightfall, the fish trap disgorged another windfall. Spirits soared, and the feast was prepared at the big campfire. The meat was broiled on the coals, the fish encased in mud and baked. Flour from Fort Boise combined with odd meat cuts for dumplings. Pooled coffee filled a tub. They ate to the point of disgorging. As if to acknowledge the occasion, the sky cleared. The stars came out. Music struck up, and the dance began on the wet grass of the Grand Ronde.

Nobody minded what discomfort there was. Shouts passed back and forth, laughter bucketed about. "If we had a jug," a man bawled, "I'd say we'd took the wrong turn somewheres and stumbled onto Heaven!"

Starbright watched his chance and finally

cut in on Rita. He said, "Whenever we've had a dance before it's led to something between you and me."

"Won't any more," said Rita. "I don't trust you. I detest you."

But she danced with him as impartially as with the other men. She did not favor Tyre Redburn, though Redburn could dance again. No longer did he stand on the sidelines with his intense and bitter brooding. He was a whole man, a well man, and he watched his rival with bright and thoughtful eyes.

He's wondering if he's strong enough, thought Starbright. *When he figures he is, he'll have to have it.*

The reflection lifted the recklessness in him. To Rita he whispered, "I'm going down to the fish trap."

"Why tell me?"

"Thought you might like to know." He saw uncertainty flicker in her firelit eyes.

He sauntered off at the end of that dance number. A roaring stimulation was in him again. At the trap he found a dry place under a pine and seated himself there, the music now a distant pleasantness, the wet earth giving up its rich smells. He waited half an hour then at last knew that someone was coming toward him along the river bank. He couldn't see yet but his breath caught, a wild elation running through him.

He gave a start when he saw two figures

shape up from the obscurity of the brush, a woman but also a man. They came on, closer to the water than Starbright. They made their way on to the trap and halted. An acid washed through Starbright; it localized in a heated prickling on his face and forehead. The pair was Rita and Redburn. As Starbright watched them, he saw them turn together, their figures blending.

He saw Redburn hungrily drink of Rita, her shape fused to his. He saw the man's hands stroke her back. He saw them move on into obscurity again, Rita now towing the man by the hand.

Murder exploded in Starbright. Redburn did not know he was near, but Rita did. But the man wasn't going to be stopped by any shake of the head. Rita was wise enough to realize the heat of the fire with which she played. She had wanted Starbright to see and relied upon his nearness to protect her from Redburn's crowding hunger. She expected it to be broken up, was forcing Starbright to do so. He swore softly. She was succeeding, for Starbright couldn't stand the thought of leaving her to Redburn. She would have a fight, for she had led the man on too far.

Starbright cut about them through the trees and was seated on the bank when they came along. Rita gave a genuine cry of surprise. Redburn said something sharp and inaudible.

"What you doing off here?" asked Starbright. "Hunting a land claim?"

Rita's head tossed. "If so, we'll have to look farther for one we like. Come on, Tyre." They did not stop. Starbright watched them disappear again into the lower brush.

For a moment he could only stand with rage boiling through him. He was damned if he would fish her out again. Swinging about, he started back toward the wagon camp. He did not rejoin the dance but went directly to his own camp where he could watch the river bank. He seated himself by the cold fire and pulled out his pipe. Wagner was over at the dance, which now had become an annoyance to Starbright. He realized that he was moved by jealousy to the point of running wild. Yet he admitted that he had forced her on down the river with Redburn.

Starbright sat there for what he thought was unending hours before he saw them coming back, slowly and holding hands. He remembered how he had been warned that he was driving her into the man's arms. *Well, you done it,* he told himself and he moved back into concealment from them.

The train encamped the second day, although Starbright was unable to contain his wild energies. He left Lafferty at the camp and rode forward to prospect the trail soon to lift into the Blue Mountains. He spent the day at it and, as he returned, watched black clouds drift in across the sky. It was a solid overcast and meant a drenching rain. It might, he realized, mean snow for them in the mountains.

Thereafter the wagon train made its way along the river toward the Blues and the pass to the Walla Walla. There was rain all through the valley and, the night before they reached the divide, they got snow. There wasn't much, but the camp roused the next morning to a whitened world, to a sloppy trail through the aisles of the evergreens.

The country was rugged, giving the wagons endless trouble. It snowed again and heavier on the second day, and snow dusted them all the way down the mountains. But the hardened train had not dropped a wagon when it came at last upon the upper Walla Walla.

The first night after the Blues were put behind, Lafferty sought Starbright. He said, "Well, it's going to be. She told the women in our camp. There'll be a wedding when we hit the mission."

Starbright's mouth gave a twist. "Time, maybe," he snorted.

Lafferty looked at him closely. "She knew Ruby'd tell me and I'd tell you. She wants you to break it up, man."

"Tired of that," Starbright returned.

Lafferty began to look angry. He said, "White women and squaws, they're alike. And I know a little about 'em. But you,

Starbright — you don't know your ear from a hole in a stump."

"Know when I'm well off," said Starbright.

"All right," said Lafferty. "You don't want her. She's too much for you to handle, so you'll turn her over to Redburn. But he won't have her, Starbright. Not with what I know about that man."

"How you going to help it?"

"I hoped," Lafferty exploded, "that you would."

With frowning eyes, Starbright watched Lafferty walk away. The man's news had set concern churning in him although he had been told by Rita herself that it would happen. For a long moment he stood shaking his head.

The wagons moved on down the Walla Walla, finding it easy going after the Blues. They were again in sagebrush country, rolling and otherwise bare plateaus. Starbright had conceived a plan, and now he hurried the wagons. And it came about that they camped one night in a position where the next day's travel would take them well past the mission. He had an asset now in the haste of the company to reach Fort Walla Walla and its boats.

"Mission's for Injuns," he told his people, "and a little out of our way. They got nothing for us, anyhow. There's nothing we need as bad as time. I figure to keep right on rolling for the Columbia. There's boats there, you know. Boats for a few lucky ones."

Rita heard and frowned. Tyre Redburn heard and scowled. But the company made a chorus of its approval.

Afterward Wagner said, "Not a bad play, Starbright, but not good enough. Nothing's to keep those two from riding over to the mission, getting it done, then catching up. Don't trust it, man. You've got to come up with something better."

Starbright chewed his pipe stem for a long while. "Would you do another marrying," he said finally, "if it was me and Rita?"

"I married Lafferty, didn't I? I can distinguish between man and animal."

Starbright strode over to the Owen wagon. The Owens, the Laffertys, the Langs stared up at him and not with much surprise. Starbright thought he saw a smile form on Rita's mouth only to be pressed out flat. He nodded at the others and looked at her again.

"Come with me," he said.

"Where?"

"Anywhere. I've got to talk to you."

"Talk here."

Kelly Lang leaned forward and fixed his gaze on his daughter. In a soft tone, he said, "Do what the man said."

Rita tossed her head then came lightly to a stand. She walked off, picking her own direction, Starbright following. Presently they were walking the bank of the river.

Starbright said, "Wagner will marry you to me. But not to Redburn. Let's stand up before him." He groped and stumbled, trying to get hold of the right words. He had none that would match the feeling in him, that would describe his thoughts of her, his need.

She halted, and for a moment he thought she would turn back to the camp. But she lingered. She looked up at him. Now he placed his hands gently on her arms. He drew in a deep breath and said, "I've never wanted any thing more."

She didn't try to pull free of him. He was humble, holding back, not wanting to make a mistake with her again.

"And I've never wanted anything less," she said.

The crash he heard he knew to be in his own inner ears. She turned to leave him but he reached and caught her. He spun her about, caught and crushed her in his arms. She kicked. She struck at him with balled hands and tried to break free. Yet she was silent except for the sudden catch of her breath.

He kissed her throat, prying back her head. Abruptly he released her and said, "Now go back to camp. Get married to the man. You can't do it."

She stood still, in an intensity that was all but hypnotic.

She said, "All right. You have the power to make me feel like the four-legged female you want."

"Run," said Starbright. "Nobody's holding you here."

He was surprised when she surged toward him. She had lowered a shoulder, and she hit him hard. The wet underfooting let him down, and she fell with him. He landed hard on his back, Rita on top of him. She was striking him, clawing and drawing blood. She moaned with the rage that shook her. She had his hair, and she shoved his head again and again into the mud. Paralyzed by his astonishment, Starbright let her for a moment.

Then he gave a wrench, a twist, and rolled to turn her under. She still fought, flat on her back in the mud. It dripped from himself, and he felt the sting of her slashing fingers. She kept moaning but that, with his grunts, was still the only sound.

He panted, "This time I'll have you."

She jabbed stiffened fingers into his eyes, and he jerked back in pain. In that instant she slid from under him and got to her knees. Her hair had loosened, and she gasped her sobs. He sludged mud from his eyes and saw that she had got hold of one of his pistols, had leveled it at him.

"I'll kill you!" she gasped. "God help me, I will!"

Starbright was still half blind. He rocked forward on his knees.

"Stay away from me — !"

He threw himself toward her, and then the world blew up.

CHAPTER FOURTEEN

Starbright heard voices through the roaring in his head. Yet the roaring was less than the searing pain. He was aware of groaning, of trying to pry open his eyes. Each lid weighed a hundred pounds. He got them lifted to have firelight strike into his vision.

"Save him, Doc!" a man's voice was saying. "We got a wagon tongue waiting. By Christ, no man can jump a woman in this train and live to brag of it!"

"I'll tend to him," another man said, and that one was Redburn.

Starbright's vision focused. What he heard was jarring enough to settle his thoughts. He looked about and realized that he was back in his own camp. He saw Wagner pulling out his pipe and looking concerned. He saw Redburn, whose eyes were slits of hate. He saw Kelly Lang, puzzled and grave-faced.

Then he saw Rita, plastered from head to foot with mud.

"Well, Rita," said Wagner, "I guess it will be your decision as to who gets him, now that I'm done."

She didn't look at Wagner, at Starbright, at anyone. She said, "It wasn't what you think.

He didn't harm me. He wasn't trying to. It was a personal thing between us that had to be settled. It got settled."

The last words had a familiar ring to Starbright. Then his swimming thoughts located them. Those were the words with which he had accounted for his fight with Redburn at Pacific Springs. Rita turned and slipped away into the darkness.

One by one the set, furious faces showed bewilderment, in some was relief. The gathering began to fade away, Redburn the first to follow Rita. Lang gave Starbright a long glance before he departed.

Alone with Wagner, Starbright sat up. "What did she do to me?" he gasped.

"What do you think I bandaged your head for? She parted your hair."

"I'll be damned," said Starbright. "She shot me. Be damned if she didn't."

The train moved again the next morning, the outrage abated by the accounting Rita herself had given of the strange struggle. Before the line of march was formed, Starbright stood on rubber knees, his head sore and aching, and said to the pilot drivers: "We won't cross the river to the mission. Likely there's as good a ford farther down that would save us time."

Thereafter he sought Redburn. He said, "You've freeloaded long enough. I want you to ride scout, today. Go till noon. If it looks all right, wait for us. If you see trouble, come back."

Boze and Redburn were loading the cart. Redburn swung about angrily. "Why today?"

"Just occurred to me you're not paying your freight. What's the matter? You have other plans?"

"By God I have!" said Redburn. "Ride your own scout!"

"I gave you an order, man. You refusing duty?"

Redburn took a step closer, saying, "You know Rita and I are going to be married today. You can't stop it."

"Refusing duty?" Starbright asked softly.

"I'll make your damned scout after Rita and I get back from the mission."

"Too late," said Starbright. "Much too late. Saddle up, man, and get going."

"You tricky — !" Redburn abruptly fell silent. It seemed to dawn on him suddenly that, if he failed to obey the order, Starbright could place him under arrest and hold him in ropes until the train was well past this critical point. Redburn's fist clenched, then he said, "All right. And see if it stops me."

"Draw a horse from the herd," said Starbright.

He went to the Owen camp. That wagon was loaded, with Owen and Lafferty hooking up, the others ready to move out. Aware of

Rita's quickened interest, Starbright said, "We're keeping to this side of the river today. I sent Redburn ahead to scout. Good man. He'll find us good going."

Rita's mouth dropped open. Lafferty, listening up by the cattle, grinned back at Starbright. Kelly Lang stroked his jaw and his eyes began to glimmer.

Looking at Rita, Starbright said, "You look disappointed. Something you wanted at the mission?"

"If so," said Rita, "I'll get it."

Thereafter Starbright, sitting his horse and waiting for the pilot wagons to set the march, observed Ralph Wagner coming toward him on a horse.

"Where you going, Doc?" asked Starbright as the man rode up to him.

"By your permission," Wagner said, "I'd like to visit the mission. Feel I ought to meet Doctor Whitman. So I scrounged a horse and got Ted Bolton to drive the wagon till I get back. Is it all right?"

"Go ahead." Starbright was pleased. If Wagner was growing interested in missions again, he possibly was getting on top of his trouble. He watched Wagner ride out, then looked back to see that the lead wagons had peeled out of the circle and were on their way, the great ring slowly unwinding to become a straight line.

Tyre Redburn did not return to the train

to report any worrisome discoveries. At midday, Starbright rode forward and found the man sitting on a rock, his horse hipshot and with its head drooping. Redburn watched the train master's approach with a stony face and stormy eyes.

"Am I through now?" he said.

"No," said Starbright. He waved ahead of them. "Ride to where we'll be at sundown. If you hit trouble, come back. If not, wait."

Redburn slid off the rock, his shoulders hunched. "Why, Goddamn you!"

"Refusing duty, Redburn?"

"No," said Redburn slowly, "I'm not falling into that bear trap. It's your trick. This one is." He swung onto his horse and went forward.

In late afternoon, at a place where the river looked inviting, the train found a pointed stick thrust up to show that Redburn had crossed over. The wagons made the ford without great trouble, then were back on the regular trail. Toward sundown they came to a very good campsite Redburn had selected. He had carried out his orders meticulously.

Starbright was easing up. By then the Whitman mission was miles to the rear. There was another one ahead, the Methodist mission at the *dalles* where the Columbia entered its great gorge. That was weeks ahead, but Rita and Redburn would probably wait, and in those weeks a great deal could happen.

Two hours past nightfall, Lafferty came bolting up to the Wagner wagon. The doctor had rejoined the train in midmorning and now sat by the fire with Starbright, lost in his thoughts. Starbright had left him alone with them, hoping the man was making his peace, was again able to contemplate the life he had come west to live. Now Lafferty's disturbed face caused both men to sit up straight.

"She's gone, Starbright!" Lafferty bawled. "And so's he! She went out to count the stars and never came back. I checked at Redburn's wagon and that viper Boze laughed at me. They got horses. They're going back to the mission."

Starbright had a cold, hard knot in his stomach. "When'd you see her last?"

"Hour ago. They got a big start. Starbright, we got to stop her from marryin' that coyote. She don't really want to. But if she does, her life's gone to hell."

"I wouldn't try to stop them," said Wagner.

"God, Doc!" Lafferty protested. "She's a fine kind in spite of that bull head! If she marries him, she'll stick!"

Wagner looked at Starbright, who kept swallowing hard. He said, "You can't miss a chance to whack her. I don't suppose there's a bigger knucklehead this side of the Missouri."

"That's right," Starbright agreed.

"Then relax and let them spend the night

riding. That's all they'll get out of it. Only one man at the mission could have married them. He's not there. I was sorry to miss Doctor Whitman, but he's visiting the Spalding mission, they told me. That's up on the Clearwater. Much farther than Redburn and Rita will care to ride."

Lafferty let out an explosive breath. Starbright closed his eyes. . . .

At last the wagons rolled down upon the Columbia, the great River of the West, at its big bend. Fort Walla Walla was an old trading post of the Hudson's Bay Company. It sat on a great flat, backed by rock river cliffs. Driftwood cluttered it, making it a desirable camp that long had been used by Indians and white wayfarers.

Starbright went at once to find the factor, a man of his own kind, a buckskin man with a heavy beard. His name was Dunlap, a Scot, and he said, "You're way late. You'll have a time getting past the cascades."

"How many boats you got on hand?" Starbright asked.

Dunlap held up two fingers and said, "We hoped the emigration was over for this year. We're getting set to winter. There won't be boats up from Vancouver for a month or six weeks. Not much we can do for you."

"We got old ones and young ones," said Starbright, "and some just poorly. How many could two boats take?"

"Around eighty," said Dunlap. "And I'm getting a party ready to go up to Fort Okanogan. But all right. We'll take them down. Now tell them all to make themselves at home. They're welcome to what we have."

Starbright knew that he was in for trouble from the wagon company. Eighty boat seats to be filled from a company of over three hundred people. He was determined to select the ones to go down to the *dalles* by boat. Therefore he called a general meeting and explained the situation. The news was sullenly received. The wagon trail, which skirted the river, was of the roughest kind.

A settler hooked his thumbs beneath his belt, scanned the company with truculent eyes and said, "It looks to me like we all set out on this trail on an equal footing. The old that come, the young and weak. When they set out or were brought it was known what they faced. It was accepted. What right they got to expect special treatment? I don't see it that one's got a right another don't have."

"You want a ride, Porter?" Starbright asked.

"Hell no. But I got a wife and young 'uns. Everybody's got 'em. Mine ain't poorly. We've took care of ourselves. They ain't weak. We come with backbones. But winter's here, and it can beat the strongest man that ever lived if it catches him in the wrong place. Them as goes on the wagons will run a big risk. It's who's going to get a good chance to live and who's got to risk dyin', the way I see it. You ain't God, Starbright. I say we ought to draw lots."

"I'll fill the boat seats," said Starbright. "That is, I'll let Doc Wagner do it. The ones that need to ride. Not the ones that want to."

"Doc will have the say," Starbright insisted. "What he says, I'll say. And what I say goes."

"Maybe your say ain't the big say it was!" yelled Porter. "You never set too well with this company, in the first place. After what happened the other night up the Walla Walla, you don't set good at all. We're on the Columbia. We can't get lost now. Anyhow, it looks to me like Redburn's been ready to take his job back a long while. I say we draw lots. What do you say, Redburn?"

"That's the only fair way to do it," Redburn said readily, an amused glance on Starbright.

Wagner, beside Starbright, murmured, "Easy, Dix, he's playing politics."

Kelly Lang made a motion of disgust, looking at Porter, then at Redburn. He said, "I'm calling for a vote of confidence in Starbright."

Starbright's eyes glimmered. It was the first time Lang had thawed out since the big trouble with Rita.

Then Starbright was repressing a smile, for Lang's call brought an overwhelming response. When he called for the negative, there were less than fifty.

"All right," said Starbright. "Doc will draw up a list of the boat passengers."

Redburn stood stock still for long moments after the assembly broke up. He had suffered a stinging defeat in the company's rejection of him. He had suffered other things that already festered in him. Starbright stood watching him, feeling the raking impact of the man's eyes. Then Redburn turned away.

Lafferty came up to Starbright and said, "Long ways to the *dalles* yet, ain't it?"

"And a rough one."

"By God," said Lafferty, "watch Redburn, man."

CHAPTER FIFTEEN

The wagons trailed again the next morning. They left behind a quarter-part of the company, Wagner having made the selections. Some wagons, which had to go on by land, were left without drivers and Starbright was required to find somebody to take over. The boat party would wait behind at the fort for a few days, being able to run the distance more speedily than could the wagons. The groups would rejoin at the rapids of the *gran dalles,* far down the river.

Starbright took his usual morning scout. The trail now followed the Columbia, swinging in its great bend toward the west again, into the highlands of the Umatilla. It was open country, sage-dotted still, roughly broken by eroded rock. The last trading establishment was behind. Fort Vancouver would be the next to come, and it would mark the end of the crossing. They were close to the valley of their dreams in distance if not in point of time.

They camped close to the trail the first night out of Fort Walla Walla. Kelly Lang sought Starbright to say, "It's time I was thinking of my gold."

"Been able to forget it?" asked Starbright.

Lang grinned, saying, "Sometimes I have. I expect to get it back. But it has been good for me to be without it, to face the chance that I might never recover it. I tell you one thing. If I find myself banking in Oregon, as I intended, I'll have a better understanding of the settlers I'll deal with."

"And if you never find yourself banking?"

"Then I can become a settler myself. But right now Redburn worries me. As long as he felt sure of his ground, I figured that time was on my side. Rita would keep him on hand, and certainly he would keep the gold at hand. But he's not certain of Rita, now. That makes me uneasy about the gold."

"Ought to be certain of her," said Starbright. "She's given him plenty of reason."

"And plenty of reason to feel otherwise. He's not stupid. He knows that whenever she comes his way it's because of something between her and you. The company has repudiated Redburn. I did before that. And I think Rita did — that night back on the Walla Walla when she exonerated you."

Starbright grinned painfully. "She lied about that. I gave her reason to shoot."

"As long as she preferred to lie," Lang said, "I'll leave it between the two of you. My point is this: if Redburn decides there's nothing but the gold in it for him, he might try to make off with it."

"Where could he go?"

"California, Santa Fe."

"Wants a showdown with me, first," Starbright reflected. "Till that comes, I wouldn't worry much about him running off."

"Just the same," Lang said doggedly, "I know he's got escape in the back of his mind. I've watched him and Boze. At Fort Boise they cut open the chest in one of the mechanic shops. They managed to remove the half-melted gold. Redburn thinks I'll be watching the chest. It's that old shell game again. The gold isn't in the chest now, but as long as I think so Redburn has got an advantage. He could make off with it. He could even bury it to be picked up later. But I'm checkmated as long as Rita is determined to trust the man."

"How'll you ever claim your gold?"

"I've got to wait for the breaks, Starbright."

Starbright's eyes were narrowed in interest. Lang was guessing shrewdly, for it did look like Redburn might be preparing an escape, should he need it. He had bought horses at Boise and picked up another at Walla Walla. He was still using the cart but if need be he could pack up some night and be off, easily outdistancing the lumbering train. Yet Starbright had no feeling that Redburn was whipped yet. The man had fought hard to come back and he had come back strong. He would have to be beaten worse than the time before. To be beaten worse, he would have to be killed.

"As for you," Lang resumed, "I'd feel better if you had eyes in the back of your head. I don't think Redburn wants another fight with you — not after what happened to him the first time. I'm afraid you won't get a fair warning when he tries again."

"Doubt it, myself," Starbright admitted.

The sky was constantly leaden, and there were scattered rains. The oxen stumbled. They galled in their yokes in spite of care. Wagons skidded on the downgrades, stalled on the many climbs. Always the great river lay on the right, running under basalt cliffs, blown into chop and needled by the rain. The wagons tooled past rapids of terrifying violence, rapids that the boats would have to run.

There came a morning when Starbright kicked off damp blankets and rose miserably to face another cold, wet day. Wagner, who often awakened the earlier, still lay wrapped in his cocoon under the wagonbed. The camp was on a bald headland above the Columbia. River mist lay between it and the water, laced by rain from mantling black clouds. The trail ran on to where the benchland climbed, the ruts of the rough thoroughfare filled with muddy water.

Starbright took a second and closer look at Wagner.

"Something wrong, Doc?" he asked sharply. "You look peaked."

The wind made his voice sound hollow and all but washed the words away. Starbright got down on his knees beside Wagner. The man's eyes were underpainted with black, the balls had a lustre, and when he opened his mouth to answer his teeth began to chatter.

"I've been up a dozen times since bed-time," he said. "Diarrhea."

Starbright settled on his haunches, a rough palm stroking his bewhiskered jaw. "You got fever."

"The weather," said Wagner. "Intestinal grippe. I'll be all right as soon as I've stirred around a while."

Starbright got kindling from the sack under the wagon and started a breakfast fire. From time to time he gave Wagner's still figure a worried study. The camp came alive, its members hustling to get a fire started under the discouragement of wind and rain. The herd was on ahead, save for a small saddle band, and men went grumpily forth to orga-nize the day's dreary march. Then Wagner rose hastily from his blankets and, half dressed, hurried into the concealment of the nearby rocks.

By the time breakfasts were finished the word had spread through the train that the doctor himself was sick. Starbright knew the news had got out when the man Porter stumped

214

into the camp and said, "What's this I hear about Doc?"

"Got the scours," said Starbright.

"How do you know it ain't cholera? He's got to be quarantined. Get him out of this camp."

"Why, damn you!" said Starbright.

"Then keep him here!" Porter bawled. "And we'll get the camp away from him!" He wheeled about and plodded off.

"I won't start an epidemic," Wagner said feebly. "But hysteria could be as bad. It's just as well. I'll fall back. I guess I couldn't travel today, anyhow."

"I'll stay with you," said Starbright. He had already decided that going on today was out of the question for Wagner. He had considered holding the whole train but now dismissed that.

He found Lafferty at the Owen wagon having breakfast with his wife and in-laws and the two Langs.

"You got promoted," Starbright told Lafferty. "You're taking the train on."

"Heard they're saying Doc's got cholera," Lafferty said. "That's given a lot more the drizzles. You falling back?"

"That's right."

"So'll I. This knot-headed company couldn't get lost now if it tried. There's a river to follow clean to the valley."

"You'll do what I said."

215

"There's Umatillas around here, Dix. Give any breed of Injun a chance at a lone wagon, and he's apt to hone his scalping knife."

Owen said, "We'll fall back with our wagon, and that'll make two of 'em. And women to cook. Doc needs fresh meat. Anyhow soup. Man might get antelope around here. Anyhow, jackrabbit. We'll fall back, Starbright." He looked at Lang. "If it's all right with you folks to pack on by yourselves."

"I'd like to stay, too," Rita said. Her father nodded.

Starbright felt something warm touch his heart. This party had not panicked. He smiled and said, "What Doc's got is a thing that needs privacy. Seen a lot of it. Only lasts two-three days. You people go on, and thanks. We'll catch up at the *dalles*."

Yet it gave Starbright an odd feeling to see the train go on. The one wagon, alone on the tramped expanse of the vanished camp, seemed pitifully small and feeble. But Wagner was too sick to care much himself.

Starbright rustled about for what firewood he could find, abandoned at deserted campfires. He yoked up the oxen and moved the wagon crosswind, then drifted the beasts out to graze again. He built a new fire to leeward of the wagon, and he took a spare wagon sheet and set it up to make a canopy. He dried out his own blankets, then had Wagner change beds.

"Glad the train's gone," said Wagner. "Now I don't have to go so far into the rocks."

"If you can make out, I'm going to see what I can shoot."

"All I need's a clear runway. Go on."

Starbright saddled his horse and rode directly south. The country was all but bare, but as the train had come into the palisades it had caught glimpses of pronghorn antelope, too distant and speedy to be easy targets from the moving train. Now Starbright set himself to find one such band.

He rode for two hours, pushing ever closer to the distant mountains, before he got his chance. Topping a rise, he looked down a sharper decline to see a band of six or seven of the lightning swift little animals below. They were upwind and had caught neither sound nor scent of him. Starbright swung his horse back hastily and dismounted. Leaving the animal, he began to slip forward, the rise between him and his quarry.

He measured the distance carefully and when he thought the time was right he bent and prowled again to the summit. His breath caught and, straightening, he lifted the rifle and fired. The gun exploded. Half a dozen tawny, horned shapes whipped into action. But one went down at the end of a single bound. Whooping, Starbright rushed down upon it to slit its throat.

He rode in with the whole carcass, feeling

cheered. Wagner showed little interest, but Starbright hung the carcass to the hind end of the wagon, dressed and skinned it out. He had not yet taken time for his own breakfast. He cooked it while he boiled up a meat broth for the doctor. The meat took longer to cook. He ate and finally filled a cup with the broth.

"You don't want it," he said. "But you've got sense enough to know you need it."

"I've swallowed a quart of bismuth," said Wagner. "This'll make it a glue." He emptied the cup and laid back.

By late afternoon Wagner had quit cramping and running for the rocks. He took broth frequently and in addition gave himself medicines from his bag. At dusk he fell into a long, unbroken sleep.

The camp had been made comfortable and Starbright sat by the fire smoking his pipe. He kept remembering the ready way the Owen party had offered to fall back with them, nobody knowing for sure but what Wagner could spread a deadly contagion. The wind had died, and he could hear the river running below him. At last, assured that Wagner was sleeping restfully, Starbright turned in.

His awakening was rude, without preparation. The moon was lost behind black clouds. Wind and rain had resumed in the hours he had slept and their noise had denied his ears

a warning. His first split second of consciousness told him he was still hearing the crack
of a gun. The two beds were under the fly,
between the wagon and dead fire. A bullet
had hit metal on the wagon's running gears
and howled away.

Kicking out of his blankets, Starbright realized what had saved him or Wagner from
being its target. There was now silence in
which the rifleman — red or white — reloaded. The fellow believed them to be
sleeping under the wagon, had not come
close enough to detect the difference. He
moved to the front of the wagon.

Fire made its burst out over him, higher
even than a standing man, the fellow apparently sitting a horse to shoot, prepared for
flight. An Indian, perhaps, but Starbright
thought otherwise. A day's march for the
wagons would be only a couple of hours' ride
for a man on a good horse. Starbright had a
feeling that this one was from the settler
camp, wherever it was tonight, and that his
work was to be called that of the Indians if
successful.

Starbright threw a shot at the place where
he had seen the gunflash. The action made
him a target but it also drew the fire away
from where Wagner lay. He could not discern
its effect. The other man was reloading, and
Starbright kept his second shot for quick use
when he saw the next gunflash.

It did not come. Starbright still could not make out a shape in the rain-slashed blackness before him.

The only way to find out was to investigate the forward area. Moving back to the protected side of the wagon, Starbright came to a full stand and moved the length of the vehicle. He found nothing.

Starbright returned at last to Wagner. He said, "Redburn or Boze. This gave them their opportunity."

"See them?"

"No," said Starbright. "But I can find out when we catch up with the train. Whoever was on stock guard tonight will know who got a horse."

"Then what?" Wagner asked softly.

"When I know, I've got a man to kill. I almost did the other time he tried for me. I come to regret that I didn't."

"You know enough about him to ruin him, don't you?"

"More than enough," said Starbright.

Wagner made a long sigh. "I think some of it has to do with Liz."

"What if you were sure?"

"If I were sure that he had anything whatsoever to do with what happened to her, I'd kill him, Starbright."

"He's my meat, Doc. You forget it."

"Then he did."

CHAPTER SIXTEEN

By morning Wagner felt strong enough that he insisted that they go on. Starbright agreed to do it only if the doctor would ride in the wagon. Thereafter Starbright broke camp, spanned up the oxen, tied his horse behind the wagon and drove out along a wet and lone pair of tracks. Fury went with him. Redburn had lost his taste for an open showdown. He was fighting now any way he could to retain what he had gained, to secure what he had hoped to gain. But Starbright had what he needed to brace the man and force him into the open. A rider could not leave a wagon camp in the night any easier than one could slip away from a military encampment.

Through a storm-torn day Starbright trudged beside the wagon. The next morning he got out his moccasins to relieve his aching feet, preferring their sogginess to the pound and uncertainty of hard heels. The trail had split off from the river, feeling its way into the shallow canyons. Early that morning the wagon growled down into a wide sandy hollow, where earth traceries announced that the main train had found hard going. He picked his own way across the flat and, with

Wagner still within the wagon, pushed on into late evening, coming then onto the highland above a deeply dug creek.

Leaving the wagon, Starbright walked forward to a high point, staring below. Cutting across the high plains in its search for the Columbia, the creek ran far down from him between rusty cliffs. The trail, pushing due west here, struck down to the narrow creek valley to make the ford, then gave a hard, right-hand heave to the top again.

Going back to the end of the wagon, he called, "How you feeling, Doc? We got a piece of hard going ahead. Might be safer, and a damned sight more comfortable, if you walked."

Wagner's head appeared through the back canvas. He looked worn, and the three days of illness had wasted him surprisingly. He glanced about him, unmindful of the rain that pelted his head. Smiling at Starbright in a tired way, he said, "I've progressed from sick to lazy. Walking would be good for me." He disappeared to emerge fully clad and let himself down carefully to the ground.

At the top of the decline Starbright locked a wheel with a chain. Even then the slippery mud caused the wagon to yaw and groan as it rumbled down. But they came into the valley's narrow confines without trouble and there made camp.

After supper Wagner pulled out his pipe,

the first time he had shown a taste for to-bacco since the start of his trouble. After-ward, smoking with the doctor, Starbright felt cheered. Wagner was well on the road to re-covery. By the time they caught up with the wagon train, he would be back on his feet.

Finally Wagner said, "I don't know how to tell you that I appreciate your help."

"Forget it."

"I don't want to. There are things a man wishes to forget. But, thank God, there are also things he likes to remember."

The high plain grew rough again. They crossed a deep dry canyon in midmorning and not long afterward came to yet another canyon into which the trail dropped to stay for many miles. They nooned briefly at the site of what had been an overnight camp for the party, perhaps last night's. Wagner had walked through that morning, and he seemed more restored than tired by it although they had bucked a steady rain.

Their cold meal finished, Wagner said, "I can handle the wagon from here on. The trail's certainly marked plain enough. You go on. I know you're anxious to get back with the company."

"Gaining on it right along," said Starbright and refused to entertain the suggestion.

The trail swung with the canyon in a gradual southward bend. They came pres-ently to a small stream that entered and ran on with them. Shortly afterward Starbright grew aware of a beat in the storm racket and abruptly halted the wagon to listen. In a moment he was certain that a horse was coming toward them, ridden hard.

"Be from the train, wouldn't it?" Wagner asked.

"Likely. But Canadian trappers come through here, too."

Within minutes a running horse came out of the slot where the bend seemed to make a solid wall. With the storm in his face, the rider bent forward, low on the animal's back. Then something caused him to look up, and he abruptly lifted an arm and waved it above his head.

"Mountain trick," said Starbright. "That's Lafferty with steam up. Something went wrong."

The horse splattered on to the wagon. The wind on Lafferty's open mouth made him seem to gasp. He gave no greeting, crying, "God, am I glad to see Doc up and going! We had trouble!"

"What?" Starbright thundered.

"A wagon. Owen's. It went over this morning in a canyon. It caught Owen under it. He's all but done for."

"Make it, Doc?" asked Starbright.

"Certainly."

"Then take my horse."

Wagner swung into the wagon to get what

he would need. Starbright untied the horse from the hind end and threw on the saddle while Lafferty slipped the bridle on. Starbright realized that Lafferty was shaken beyond wanting to talk and did not pry at him with questions. At last Lafferty spoke again.

"This canyon comes into another, pretty soon. And a bigger crick than this. It's rocky as hell in that canyon. Up and down. I rode the length of the thing before the train started in. The boulder that ruined Owen must of rolled onto the trail right behind me. Owen, he was pilot wagon. He come down around a sharp turn and seen this big rock. Mud wouldn't let him stop. Tried to swing out enough to pass but the damned wagon yawed hard and tipped over. Caught him."

"The others?" Starbright asked, thinking of Ruby and Rita and the rest of that party.

"Walking. They're all right. But Owen — hell. Both legs busted and torn. His chest smashed to hell and gone. He ain't got a chance, but the women wanted Doc. Owen — he's been as close to a daddy as I ever had."

"How far?"

"Eight, ten miles. We made camp. You can get there by dark."

Wagner had gone up to the saddle. Abruptly he and Lafferty rode out. They went swiftly, the horses throwing mud, and at last were swallowed by the bend.

Starbright had a sudden sense of being alone in a hostile world and it startled him. Only weeks ago he had been a trader, a buckskin man, as at home on the solitary trails as elsewhere, rarely lonely and never knowing a need for others about him in order to feel right. But he was not displeased by the discovery. A man wanted his kind. He was built to live as a member of some group, to be a contributing part in some common effort.

Starbright forged on into late day, into early dusk. He was now down upon the rocky creek Lafferty had mentioned, moving west again. Winking firelight, far ahead on the thin flat of the creek, told first of the train. It gave him relief but failed to cheer him because he knew that he was only coming into sadness.

The train had been forced to make camp in a drawn-out line, all down the length of the canyon. The pilot wagon, early that day, had made one of the many climbs and come down upon disaster and blocked the trail. Starbright passed the loose stock and pulled up at the end of the train and was greeted by a number of people who had expected and heard him coming on. One of these was Kelly Lang.

"How's Owen?" Starbright asked, and that was their only greeting.

"Holding on. And I say more's the pity."

"No chance?"

"Wagner doesn't think so."

Disaster had brought out of the party a deep hunger for action and distraction. Somebody was unhooking Starbright's steers, then taking them on the herd. A woman told him to come over to her fire for his supper. But he walked forward with Lang. The Owens were at the head of the train, and that was nearly a mile on down the canyon.

A tent had been set up at the head of the train, a campfire built in front of it. A score of people were about the fire, helpless, anxious and waiting. Starbright saw Rita at the blaze with Ruby and the other Owen girl. For an instant Rita's eyes met his and she smiled gravely, and he had the sure knowledge that there was relief in her at seeing him again. The Owen girls were dry-eyed, silent. They waited, as did the others. Mrs. Owen was with a group of older women and Lafferty, wearing a deep scowl, stood off to himself.

Starbright walked up to him, reached out and cuffed his arm. "Keep your chin up, man."

"Hell," Lafferty said, "he ain't even unconscious. He's got to lay there feeling it. Waiting to die. He's been at it ever since it happened this morning. Just waiting to die."

"Maybe not," said Starbright.

"Why maybe not?" Lafferty whirled on him. "Doc says he'd have to take off both legs if Owen lives. Why not die? Why not, God damn you?"

Abruptly Starbright himself was wholly helpless. He had come to the end of action, and the sudden lack of anything further that he might do became at once a burden. He flung a glance at the lighted tent and could see a shadow moving beyond and knew that the shadow was Wagner. He knew also that Wagner had done all he could by now and was himself reduced to waiting.

Presently a woman walked from the group about Mrs. Owen and went to the tent flaps where she halted uncertainly. She lifted a hand as if to knock on the tent pole, then the arm fell slack at her side. She said, "Some of us think we ought to pray, doctor."

The shadow of Wagner did not move.

"You lead us in it?" she asked, faltering. Then she turned back.

Somebody was tugging at Starbright's arm. He looked down to see a woman with a cup of steaming coffee. He took it gratefully and let it burn as he emptied the cup. But it failed to cut the cold in him and he knew that nothing would except the passing of this situation.

A man walked up to the Owen women and pulled off his hat. He said, "I ain't much good praying. I been a ornery cuss and I reckon I lack the pull. But I'll try." A group pressed in about them, enlarging, cutting them off from Starbright's sight.

Lafferty said, "Pray, hell. Why don't Doc give him something to put him out of his misery?"

Starbright at last entered the tent. Wagner looked up with a frown, recognized him and let his face relax. They had set up a cot for Owen. He was covered by blankets, the lantern light showing his twisted face and staring eyes. Starbright walked over and stood above the man. Owen seemed not to recognize him.

Moving back, Starbright whispered, "Prayers out there. Medicine in here. And you seem to be sticking with the medicine."

"Not so far apart, maybe."

"You heard Lafferty talk?"

"Yes."

"Why not do it his way? That's the step I'd take."

Wagner made a tired motion with his hand, himself not a well man. "Why have any attitude?"

Starbright tipped his head toward Owen. "He got one?"

"Lafferty's."

Yet Owen could not die, and Starbright learned that fact well as the hours wore by. The heart had gone out of Owen, the will to live had been replaced by the will to die. But the stringy, mashed flesh would not die. Once Starbright had seen a strapping man kicked a glance blow on the head by a horse. The man had dropped dead in his tracks. But this ruined, pain-frought flesh lived stubbornly, some spirit beyond Owen's control refusing extinction. Those who now prayed steadily believed this lingering to be in answer. Then in the late night Owen rallied, and at dawn he died.

His wife stood in the wet gray light and pulled herself straighter. Lafferty, looking eased, crossed to her. He said, "You ain't left without a man. As long as I live and you live I'll take care of you and Edith. Don't you fret."

"I ain't fretting," the woman said.

CHAPTER SEVENTEEN

The way was cleared, Owen's wagon righted and its load straightened out. His canvas-wrapped body was lowered into a wet grave. Wagner made a brief prayer before the man was sealed away from the living world. It was something memorized, something that did not come out of Wagner, personally.

The wagons went on, fording the John Day, then were again upon the high plains and moving back toward the river palisades. The quick, shattering way in which Owen had been taken, coming when it did, had removed from Starbright's mind his fury against Redburn, his resolve to have it out with the man. But now he made investigations. He ran down the man who had been on stock guard at the approximate time he believed Redburn had got a horse to leave the train. That man had been Cob Boze. It was useless to question him, but that fact alone confirmed Starbright's suspicions. Yet he lacked a solid ground for bracing his enemy.

The rain drizzled off but the strong winds blew continually on the plateaus. They were mainly from behind the march, as if warning the company of winter and hurrying it on toward the Cascades barrier. They cut through clothing and flesh to reach up the very marrow of the bone.

Then the train came down to the Deschutes crossing to face an awesome headland to be surmounted in order to circumvent the *dalles,* cascades, and the falls that ran for the next fourteen miles. But the arrival was an accomplishment, for here the boat parties from Fort Walla Walla would rejoin the train. The wagons reached the point too late in the day to tackle the hill. Starbright ordered camp and had the herd drifted back onto the river flat behind them.

A big island stood off in the river from the camp. On the distant shore ran a bare mountain while on the near side the naked headland bulged in to create the first jaws of the long river gorge. The grinding of the falls came to the company and was a steady background to the racket of the camp.

Starbright felt impatience. The feeling had a hook and got hold of his old impulsive aggressiveness. He went to the Owen camp, which now was in the charge of Lafferty. Rita was helping the other women start a meal over the open fire, although hours of daylight remained.

"Want to see a sight?" Starbright asked her.

"What?"

He grinned. "Still expect me to sell you a

pig in a poke, huh? I've heard tell that the Injuns have a fishery at the falls. Not far to walk, if you'd like to stretch your legs some more."

"They're stretched," said Rita, "till I feel a mile high. But I'd like to see it."

She got a coat and wrapped a kerchief about her head. Watching, Kelly Lang looked interested. This was the first time Starbright had sought her since the night when she had all but blown off his head. Lang seemed as relieved as Starbright to find that she was not nursing a grudge.

They struck off together, Starbright shortening his stride to match the girl's. A river flat lay under the headland, swinging forward to a sharp cliff, and they used the flat while skirting the bare lift of the big hill. The wind brisked as they came closer to the portal, the roar of the falls — still well below them — increasing. Then they rounded the cliff and pressed on for another considerable distance to find themselves halting on a river bluff dropping hard to a tortured river bed.

"It's frightening," said Rita.

The river below them was shredded into several savage channels that howled and brawled between vast upthrusts of basaltic rock. Far on the north side were the vaguely recognizable shapes of an Indian encampment, with more lodges scattered without order on this side. At a distance downstream showed the curving, rushing lips of the falls, which stretched from shore to shore.

From the rock on the shore and even from the broken rock islands, fishing platforms thrust out over the swirling water, threatening where a minor falls broke one of the near channels. Wishram Indians stood upon the platforms, fingers glued to the handles of the dipnets with which they swept the channels. Rita squealed and pointed as a buck directly under them brought up his net hand over hand to reveal a wriggling salmon enmeshed.

But Starbright's study was mainly upon the openmouthed girl. The weeks had changed her, sobering and perhaps deepening her, and he had a sudden feeling that she had spent herself against him in that last violence as he was spent against her. Oddly at this moment he had no desire to touch her, to do more than watch her, and suddenly he understood what she had meant when she had denied his possession of tenderness. *You pull too hard, then you hit too hard.* . . . Suddenly there was great regret in Starbright.

Everywhere below them the Indians were taking up their fish from the river, laboring steadily, for the run was seasonal and the season was at its end.

"What a savage river," Rita said. "And we've got to ride it — how many miles?"

"Fifty, sixty," said Starbright. "Scared?"

"You know better than that."

"Reckon I do."

He was searching his mind hard to find the right thing to say to her to preserve this pleasant moment in her mind. All through the last days he had become more and more aware of the fact that another church mission lay close ahead of them, at the place where the train would break up and take to raft. Once up the big hill, that wasn't much more than a day's march for the wagons. Yet he could not bring himself to allude to it, to try to feel out her intentions.

Finally he said, "We've come a long piece together, haven't we?"

"I'm glad it will soon be over. For a long while the trail thrilled me. It stirred things I didn't know were in me. But I'm tired of those things. I want rest and peace and quiet. I want work and something that won't change except to grow."

"Got it planned very close?" he asked cautiously.

"Yes. Definitely."

And then they went back to the wagon camp.

That evening the boat parties got in from Fort Walla Walla. In the morning the wagons started over the big hill. It was an enormous, grueling climb. A wagon at a time went up under all the draft that could be hooked on, its wheels blocked and reblocked as it went forward foot by foot. All that day was required to form the train again at the top of the headland.

Lafferty looked back at the deep cut of the wheels and said, "Damme, we grooved that hill till it looks like a fat woman's bottom."

Camp that night was scarcely two miles from the previous one, and that night snow sifted down upon the party as it slept. On the following day the march was resumed, a no more difficult trail now than countless stretches behind, yet a trail far more exacting than had been foreseen by the worst pessimist back on the Missouri. The last light had gone when the pilot wagons rumbled down hill onto the great rock-scabbed semicircle below the *dalles.*

The slushy snow had stopped before morning to be followed by a slanting rain. Wind howled in the narrowing gorge on to the west. It drove the rain against the marchers. Then a final camp was built upon the forested flat just short of the portal.

This was the end of the Oregon Trail. The distance from here to the valley of the Willamette would be covered by water. The train would break up as a single company, dissolving into rafting parties that could be comprised of no more than one or two families, with a wagon bed to hold possessions and furnish shelter.

Aching in his tiredness, Starbright felt relief

that his responsibility as captain had been discharged, more fully than he had once intended, as fully as any man could ask. "They're on their own, Doc," he told his campmate. "Do you and me go down this little crick together?"

"Hoped you'd want to," Wagner admitted.

"We'll get somebody to run our stock over the Indian trail," said Starbright. He would have preferred to tend to that himself. But Wagner had a wagon to think of, with its load of possessions he had brought all the long way. He would have to raft or abandon wagon and load at this late point. He could throw in with some other party, but Starbright felt this one lingering responsibility.

Disintegration had already started work with the company. No wagon circle was formed here, individuals pulling into whatever shelter could be found among the rocks and trees. Each party chose a small length of water front for itself where a raft could be built. The forest's ragged edge showed the stumps where logs had been cut for many other rafts before, and the earth revealed the scouring where they had been dragged down to the Columbia.

Now campfires glowed and guttered in the rain. Looking about in the misty, gathering darkness, Wagner said, "I sort of hate to see it. People can't live together as we have and not grow attached."

"Or to hate each other," said Starbright.

The next morning work began in the continuing rain. Axes rang out at the forest edge. Ox teams dragged the logs across the slippery earth. Tension climbed in the company. The river was more fearsome now that they were about to launch themselves upon it. Yet launch themselves they must for there was no other way to the valley if they were to take their precious belongings, and winter pressed them from behind.

Starbright wondered why man, in his eternal restlessness, had not grown wings. Man was limited by two short legs and had rebelled against that restriction. He had claimed the earth, although it exhausted him to possess it.

The church mission that Starbright could see in the misty distance strongly drew his thoughts. Considering Rita and Redburn, he at last came to the point of decision and made it very flat finality. He could not and would not prevent their marriage through his own violence. He would not do it, even, through the charges he could make and verify by Lafferty and Wagner as to The Pheasant and the hunting knife that Wagner had found in the South Pass sage. A marriage had to happen or fail to happen through the choice of Rita, herself, if she was to be at peace about it.

Lafferty came bolting through the camps

the next morning before Starbright left for the woods with Wagner to start work on their raft. Lafferty, deeply upset, flung his voice forward.

"Redburn was at our camp just now, Dix! He's fetching the mission preacher to hitch him up with Rita!"

Starbright felt the clutch of dread in his shoulders. He murmured, "And what does the lady say about that?"

"Rita wasn't there," Lafferty said, coming up. "Her and Kelly went for a walk. Redburn, he left word with Ruby. He's crowdin' it hard. Wants to trail to the valley and start right now. Rita come back but ain't saying if she'll have the skunk."

"Well, it's *her* say," Starbright reminded.

"With her blind as a mole?" Lafferty retorted. He made a pleading motion at Wagner. "Doc, you might have influence with the mission parson! Go tell him why you wouldn't marry them two, yourself. Likely that would stop him, too. That girl's letting herself be carried into it because of this bull-headed jackass here!"

Wagner shook his head. "I felt I had a right to refuse them, Lafferty. Otherwise, it's not for me to interfere."

Lafferty blew out an exploding breath. "Right or wrong, I got the gall! I'll tell her a thing or two! If that don't work, I'll get my gun and kill him!"

"Tell her what, Lafferty?" Wagner asked in a subdued voice.

"About The Pheasant and Liz Templeton!"

"Lafferty, shut up!" Starbright barked.

"Shut up, hell!"

Wagner's face had turned to stone. He took a quick step toward Lafferty, saying, "Go on! Go on, I tell you! I've got to know!"

"All right," Starbright said angrily. "Go on and speak your piece."

"Well," Lafferty said, watching Wagner and frightened by the intensity in what had seemed so gentle a face. "Well, Doc, I wasn't thinking so much of you as of Rita. It ain't nice. You know how Redburn spent a couple of years in the high country. Well, there was a Injun princess to fill any man's eye. They ain't to be had for any pouch of beads. But Redburn, he up and helped himself. Then he skinned out. If he'd of married her, it might have been all right with her father. But his leaving her turned the chief into a fury."

"And then," Wagner said. "And then — ?"

"You've guessed it, Doc. That son-of-a-bitch, he come back leading a wagon company."

"It was revenge?"

"Doc, you hadn't ought — !"

"Redburn knew it could happen but let it happen?" Ralph Wagner's eyes had taken on a strange lustre. His thin shoulders showed his terrible awareness of the truth.

"So stop him from bringing ruin to Rita, too, Doc!" Lafferty pleaded.

Wagner's jaw muscles pouched his cheeks as he flung a slow stare from one mountain man to the other. Slowly he shook his head. "No — no. Rita's seen all that I've seen, and it was *almost* enough to tell me what you've confirmed. God himself can't save her from folly unless she's wise enough to see it for herself. No, Lafferty, I'll have no part in breaking it up."

"And *you* won't," Starbright said to the other mountain man.

Lafferty's mouth made a gasping motion. New anger streaked his eyes and went away. He said, "I'm damned if I'll watch it happen," and walked down toward the river.

But Starbright could not keep his own eyes off the log building in the far distance. Presently he saw two figures emerge, one of them Redburn. The two men struck off on a slant and disappeared among the rocks and the other wagon camps. Starbright's ears swelled to the thunder of his own surging blood.

He snapped, "What we standing here for? Let's get to work."

Wagner shook his head. "Not yet, Dix. Have faith."

An hour, or a thousand wearing, despairing years went by for Starbright. Then he saw the man returning alone to the mission, walking without haste, the need for him past. Starbright swung away and knew that if the newlyweds stayed here a single night there would be a killing. He yearned for Redburn's life with a ferocity he had not known was in him, and he knew what heated the brains of stags when they locked themselves in a fight to the death over a doe.

"Easy, Dix," said Wagner. "Kelly Lang's coming. And from the swing to him, he's not unhappy."

Starbright spun about. Lang came on across the soggy flat. Noting that he was being watched, he shoved both arms upward in a gesture of rejoicing.

"She never done it!" yelled Starbright. "Doc, she's still free!"

"Now, *I'm* at *your* service, Dix," Wagner said, grinning.

"She wouldn't have me. She hates the sight of me."

"A pity you can't match her in discernment, my friend."

Kelly Lang was smiling broadly as he came up to the camp. "You've guessed," he said.

"Flat and final?" Wagner asked.

"Yes. She apologized to the missionary for Redburn's assuming too much."

"And Redburn?"

"What does he always do when he's crossed?" Lang asked. "He turned nasty, and thank God for that because I've needed

Rita's help. I'll get it now. And I need you two, as well."

"The showdown?" Starbright asked.

"He'll clear out now. It looked to me, when I passed, like he and Boze are already breaking camp. There's only the gold for him now, and he'll fight for that."

"What's your stand?" asked Starbright.

"Logic, Dix," Lang said readily. "The company knows that the gold in question has to be his or mine. There's no way now that I can furnish proof that it's mine. But I hope to prove that it can't be his. Under the circumstances that would make it mine. You're still the train captain, Dix, and you've got the power to arrest Redburn, order a trial, and appoint a court."

"What you going to charge?"

"Murder and the robbery that motivated it."

"That'll hang him," said Starbright. "That's too easy, to my mind, but I reckon we've got to be satisfied with it. You pick enough settlers to make up a court and bring 'em to Redburn's camp. I'll go there now and see that they don't run out on it."

Kelly Lang moved off swiftly. Wagner shook his head at Starbright's glance of inquiry, understandably wanting no part in the coming events. Thereafter Starbright moved casually through the camps toward Redburn's own.

As he neared he saw that horses had been brought up. Two were saddled for riding while the others wore pack saddles. Packs had been made up of the cart's contents, and Redburn and Boze were starting to lash them to the wooden saddles.

"Rest yourselves, boys," said Starbright. He had his thumbs hooked in his belt but his hands were not far from his pistols. "It happens that you're under arrest."

Redburn straightened from a rope he was knotting. Hatred swirled in his eyes, while shock starched his cheeks. He had not expected anything as curt, as deadly as that.

"Just who are you?" he thundered.

"Train captain," said Starbright. "Remember? There's maritime law on the prairies, and you know it well. Stand still, boys. As a private citizen, I'd admire to gut-shoot you both."

"What's the charge?" breathed Redburn.

"Murder and robbery. One and the same. You'll swing for the murder, but Kelly Lang's got his gold coming back to him."

Boze swallowed hard, and Redburn's own agitation was as badly displayed. Redburn swung his burning gaze from Starbright toward a group that came across the flat toward this camp, a score of settlers with Kelly and Rita Lang among them. It was a cogent, awesome sight, and Starbright's mistake was in looking that way, himself.

It was Cob Boze who mustered the

courage to pull his pistol. Starbright found himself covered, caught flatfooted. It had seemed logical that they would make a claim to the gold they had coveted so long, which Lang could not claim except through the evidence of circumstance. Redburn might have preferred that course, but Boze lacked the nerve for it. His sudden, violent motion seemed to swing Redburn into line with his intentions.

"Trial, hell!" Boze yelled. "We're pulling stakes! Redburn, get on your horse if you're coming along! If not, you can stay and hang by yourself!"

Redburn bolted to his horse and went up to the saddle. He pulled his own pistol, turning it on Starbright while Boze mounted. His mouth made the merest, bitterest smile as he said, "Some other time, Starbright. When I hold the cards. You're not in the valley yet. You haven't married her yet. Take care, man — take care."

"Come on!" Boze screamed and thundered out.

Redburn lingered an instant longer. "Anybody who tries to follow us will die," he warned. Then the two were running their horses along the flat toward the lift of the palisades and the Indian trail to the last valley.

Coming on to the half-broken camp, Kelly Lang wore a look of amazement. "Redburn abandoned the gold?" he gasped, unable to believe it.

"Not yet," said Starbright. "He's just insuring his life, right now. Don't ever think otherwise."

He glanced at Rita, Redburn's veiled threat to her stirring a deep apprehension. She returned his study with cool, level eyes, unafraid and unwarned, yet maybe she was shrewd enough to understand that in her vanquished suitor there was now the killing, primeval rage that had filled Starbright while he waited to see if she would marry the man. That deadly, consuming emotional charge had been transferred, and to a man with less control over his actions.

"Well, it looks like that gives you a clear title to your gold, Lang," said a settler.

Kelly Lang, watching Starbright closely, showed no signs of rejoicing. . . .

As the excitement subsided, the departure of Redburn and Boze brought relief to the rest of the camp. The trail's ever-changing and ever-renewing demands quickly brought new considerations and worries to the fore. Steadily it rained and swiftly the days slid past. Axes rang out in the timber. Ox teams strained and stumbled, snaking the logs to the water.

Men formed into groups for the heavier work. Each wagon to be taken on required a raft, and there were still nearly sixty wagons in the train. The rafts had to be large enough to float both loaded vehicles and the people attached to them. They required sweeps for steering, rope oarlocks for pulling, and in some instances masts were erected for sails to take advantage of the gorge's steady wind.

Yet there was current in plenty to carry the rafts through. More often than otherwise it was excessive speed that had to be considered and countered. Worst of all would be the loneliness, each party on its own against a river greater than most of them had ever seen.

The raft-building became a grim, unannounced race. One by one, the more dexterious and hard-driving settlers began to complete their task. Then wagons were unloaded, their beds lifted off and moved aboard to serve as deckhouses for the rafts. They were reloaded, and the running gear of the wagons was knocked down and stowed wherever space permitted. The livestock was cut into bunches, with men and older boys assigned to drive them. Stock pools and rafting groups began to depart, timed to arrive together at the Cascades portage.

Starbright and Wagner were building a raft together, Lafferty and Lang another. It had been decided that the two rafts would run the gorge together, Lafferty taking the livestock, the others handling the rafts.

One by one, as they entrusted themselves

to the river, men came to shake Starbright's hand and thank him for his leadership. They were all cheerful, expecting to meet again in the valley and share many a year ahead.

Starbright did not want to rush the departure of his own group. His nerves tightened daily with the knowledge that Redburn and Boze would wait somewhere between here and the valley for a new try for the gold and revenge, as well. They had lacked time to take camping equipment and food. Redburn's experience as a mountain man would help them, but the going would be tough in this weather, and each day the ordeal was stretched out for them would weaken the pair. So Starbright took his time without communicating his reason.

CHAPTER EIGHTEEN

Early on a foggy morning, with hardly a quarter of the original company left on the flat, Starbright and group put out upon the river. The two rafts were soon reduced to dots by the towering cliffs, all but awash in the chop stirred up by the strong gorge draft. He was not a water man, nor was Lang, who managed the trailing raft. Wagner was still paired with the mountain man, while the women used the shelter of the wagon bed on the other craft.

The day's run passed without trouble. The fog lifted just enough to reveal the muddy, agitated water close about, with no glimpse of either shore. The hind raft became a ghost craft, sometimes in view and again swallowed for long hours. They passed the ingress of a river coming in from the north, steering wide of its disturbance and shoal. All day they were without a glimpse of the sky, and when a sooty stain seeping into the fog foretold of night, Starbright put in closer to the north shore. That one was safer, with the river between it and the cattle trail that had been taken by Redburn and Boze.

Presently a bulge in the shoreline showed a

flat, timbered chip of land. He ran on in, nosing against the sand. Leaping ashore, Ralph Wagner disappeared to return at once.

"A creepy place," he reported. "But as good as we'll find."

Starbright turned to yell to Lang, whose raft he could not see. He was answered, then the other craft bulged out of the mantling fog to nose in.

There was driftwood at hand. Soon Starbright had a campfire going, the others bringing up equipment for the night from the rafts. Extra wagon sheets made beds on the wet bank while the women busied themselves cooking supper. It was close quarters, with no privacy for anyone save by walking off along the rough, drenched slope of the river bank as personal comfort required.

When, lost to the outer world, the raft party had eaten, soaked up heat and dried out, a physical well-being close to gaiety rose up in its members to contradict the fog, the river and the pressing mountains. Yet, watching quietly, Starbright thought that Rita was an exception. She was quiet, lost in long thoughts, and he sensed the restlessness she harbored. Later, when he went down to check the lines of the rafts, she followed him.

"What's eating on you?" he asked.

"I don't like this."

"Is it Redburn?"

She made a quick, impatient motion. "It's

250

this. I hate tight places. Up to now we've had so much space."

"It's Redburn, I think," Starbright insisted.

"All right, have your way."

"Reconsidering?"

Her head came back. "Here we go again. What if I am?"

"You'll see him again. He's not done with you."

"Or you," said Rita. "Days we're on the river. But some night, in some camp like this, he'll come."

"It's turned into a contest as to who's going to bed with you," Starbright stated.

"I'm terribly flattered."

Starbright's own thoughts turned dark and brooding after that. What was there in love to make a man and woman so powerfully drawn and yet so utterly ruthless with each other? It was their wills, he knew, neither of them possessing the ability to bow or bend. One of them had to be the first to do it. He could not and she would not, which made them vessels shut off from fulfillment by their own flaws.

The night was clammy but the fire kept the party warm. Starbright rose before dawn and freshened the blaze for cooking purposes. He had breakfast started by the time the others roused themselves one by one, the women elbowing him back from the fire. He had all but forgotten the luxury of a woman's preparing his meals and felt strange waiting with the other men to be fed.

When they were ready to break camp, Lang said, "Dix, it seemed to me yesterday that Doc Wagner free-loaded on you all day."

"Lazy cuss," Starbright admitted.

"All day," said Wagner heartily, "I wrestled with a problem. Which was wetter, the river or the fog?"

"What you need," said Lang, "is hard, practical work. Spelling me. That sweep on my raft can fight like a bear. Dix, how about trading you a woman for him?"

"What woman you trying to get rid of?" Starbright asked.

"Not me," said Ruby Lafferty. "I'm settled on our raft." Her mother and sister shook their heads in the same way.

"That leaves you, Rita," Lang said. "I wonder how that came about?"

"Not me," said Rita. "There's not enough foot room on one of those rafts for me and Dix Starbright."

"Honey," said Ruby, "I think you'd ought to. Frankly, I don't trust your father on that sweep. Doc Wagner has more influence with the Lord."

"And I with the devil?" Rita intoned, looking at Starbright. "Ah, no, I only go from bad to worse with him."

Yet she did not object to taking place on Starbright's raft, huddled under the canvas shelter, small and miserable there, and terribly hostile. They slipped out into the fog to re-enter a world of gray oppression and of fretted water. After the departure, there was no sight of the trailing raft. Starbright began to doubt their wisdom in setting off, even though the campsite had been hardly more inviting.

Starbright remembered what Rita had said of her anxiety in restricted quarters and felt pity for her. The shelter they had rigged broke the wind but did nothing to keep out the clammy cold of the fog or to prevent the wash that ran constantly over the logs of the raft. He had a rising sense of the enormity of the Oregon emigration, of the fact that it was an undertaking stemming out of man's decisions with the women involved becoming sharers of the responsibility and ordeal with no privilege of choice.

Then, as the hours slipped by with the unseen shoreline, he began to notice how frequently she turned her attention upon the hugging hills that she could not actually see. The discernment came to him sharply that she was aware of Redburn's presence, somewhere up there in the lifts, as he was himself, and as aware of the vicious and deadly drive that now possessed the man. Gold and a woman — how much violence had stemmed from that combination!

When that charge broke and struck out like

lightning from Redburn, she would be the target as much as would Starbright, himself. Yet helplessly she must ride forward, unseeing, unknowing of what might lie in the far distance or right at hand.

He couldn't muster the talk that might comfort her, for it did not exist. The menace of Tyre Redburn was immediate and real, a fact of life. Therefore the patient arrest and waiting upon these few bobbing logs was itself wrong and treacherous. Redburn had to be killed and every instinct in Starbright warned him to seek his enemy on the offensive and get it done. That he could not do with only two other men to take care of this party, and they with even less river experience than his own.

The gorge walls seemed to be narrowing in, for sound came back louder as it rebounded from the rises. The fog did not lift, and during the whole of that day Starbright caught only glimpses of the other party, which had fallen well behind. There was nothing he could do to narrow the gap, for the current dictated the speed of both crafts. Yet as long as he knew they were safe, back there, Starbright was satisfied.

When signs of another night appeared in the fog, with the other raft lost to view again, he said, "We'll put in and trust they're trailing the shore. Then we can holler 'em down."

He headed in, calling several times and getting no response from the others. Recalling no special hazards, Starbright doubted that there had been trouble. He figured that the nearness of night would cause Lang and Wagner to skirt the shore, realizing that the lead raft would be hunting a campsite. He kept yelling while he tied up. When that brought no results, he hurried to build a fire that could be seen from out on the water.

Finally Rita said, "Let's not worry. They've had time to pass here, and they've probably done it. If we went on trying to find them, we'd pass them, too, and play leapfrog all night long. Wouldn't we?"

She was right, but now tension had got its hold on Starbright. He built the fire bigger while knowing by then that time and the current would have carried their friends on past. He could do nothing to unscramble the situation; only morning and the lifting of the fog could do that.

He shook his harried, human head and said, "We might as well eat supper."

He unloaded their requirements while Rita started cooking. They were on the same kind of gravelly talus as on the preceding night, close-hemmed by drift and broken terrain. He made their beds, one on either side of the fire, a tarpaulin folded beneath and over. He could hear the cheerful sounds of Rita's cooking, but once when he glanced at her she was staring beyond the fire before her into the concealing night.

"If there'd been trouble," Starbright said, "they'd of yelled loud enough we'd have heard it. By now they're ashore. Above or below. And probably worrying their heads off about you."

"Why me?"

"You're pinned down for the night with the devil."

"I wonder just how worried they are about that."

They ate quietly, the night by then full about them. Afterward Starbright loaded his pipe and smoked, sitting like an Indian at the fire while his boots dried at the blaze, inverted on sticks besides Rita's shoes. He kept watching the footgear, big, sturdy soles meant for striding across the world and dainty ones intended for dancing. He and Rita Lang were so utterly different, and yet he knew intuitively that this night would give her to him if he pressed.

They had let their clothing dry on their bodies, and now Rita wore moccasins that he had rummaged out of his possible bag. Presently she disappeared into the fog, returning to slip fully clad into her bed. Starbright knocked the ashes from his pipe.

He spoke across the fire to her. "I've said it before, and I say it now. I love you."

"I don't doubt that, Dix. And it's not the question."

"Our fighting is?"

"No, not that."

"You don't love me?"

There was no answer. Somewhere in the far night the wind tore sound from the forest. The river churned up its own kind of noise. But Rita had nothing to say to his question.

Starbright rose and stared across at her. The violence in his nature began to heat his brain. She lay watching him silently, without invitation and without forbidding. The decision was his, and he had a sudden knowledge that it was important to her how he made it and how he told her through his choice what he possessed of passion and of respect and restraint.

For a long moment he felt the devilish rise of urgency, of the old heedless anger against her will and wiliness. He walked over and stood above her.

He said, "Sweet dreams, my dear," and without touching her started to leave.

"Thank you, Dix," she whispered. "Now come back here. The answer is yes. I love you."

Starbright was dropping down beside her when she suddenly screamed, an abrupt and frightened scream. He had got the same bolting alarm in the split second before she cut it off, the sound of a rock rolling down the bank to *plomp* into the water. He shoved up in the firelight, fully expecting to make a target of himself but meaning to protect Rita.

He hissed to her, "Scoot — crawl out into the dark!"

She did so, knowing it was the only way she could get him to seek protection for himself. He slid on across the camp to get his gun. But by then logic had reasserted itself in his mind. He grinned but was trembling in every fiber of his body because of the raw fear he had felt for Rita.

He called, "Stay put till I make sure. Redburn couldn't get over to this side without swimming. He'll wait for the handier camps we'll have to make pretty soon." But he kicked out the fire from habit before he made his prowl along both reaches of the rough river bank.

The search reassured him. But when he returned to camp it was to find a wholly unnerved girl. Rita lay on her bed again and was crying in torn sobs that she tried to repress as he came in.

Starbright looked down at her and said, "When it clears, and we come to a good camping place, I'll leave you all there a while."

"And hunt him?" sobbed Rita.

"It's got to be. He's between us and will always be until he's dead. Wasn't that just shown to us?"

For the mood was gone from them. Tyre

Redburn had torn it away through nothing but the threat he posed to their happiness. The passion in Starbright was now the strong wish to seek a decision. He sat for a long while thinking of it while Rita, exhausted, slept.

As if Nature, herself, understood the need for visibility, the fog had lifted by morning. Starbright hurried them through breakfast and struck camp. Within the hour they were back on the river. Fifteen minutes of running showed them a campfire on the same bank they had left.

"There they are," he said. "They overshot."

"No need to put in, is there?" Rita asked hastily. "They look all right."

"We'll put in."

"Oh, Dix — you're going to leave me there with them!"

"It's best."

"Oh, no — no — !" Rita moaned and buried her face in her hands.

But she had managed to reassume a jaunty air as the raft touched the bank. Wagner and Lang waited at the water's edge, looking hale and cheerful, while the women smiled down from the camp.

"It worked, Papa," said Rita. "Now we can compel this man to marry me."

"We sure can!" Lang said heartily. "Doc, get it over before I shoot the varmint!"

Starbright jerked straight, then saw that

their very levity denied suspicions anywhere in this camp. Even Wagner was smiling, and he looked ready to get it done. Regretfully, Starbright shook his head.

"First, I've got a chore."

"Redburn?" Lang asked sharply. "Did you get wind of him?"

Starbright shook his head. "But it's plain that we're fools leaving the jump up to him. He's got two obsessions now — to get the gold, and to get even with me and you Langs. I'm going to leave Rita with you a while and go over to the south shore. I'll follow the trail to the portage. If he's not between them, he'll be there."

"Don't hunt him, Dix."

It was Ralph Wagner who spoke.

"And why not?" the mountain man demanded.

"Can't you protect your own without going out and killing what you consider dangerous to it?"

"He'll show no mercy, man!" Starbright thundered.

"And have no peace of mind — ever. He's lost the chance, Dix. But you haven't. Yet."

"If he harms Rita or even tries, I'll kill him!"

"That's different. But wait till it's inevitable."

"He's right, Dix," said Rita, and her father nodded in agreement. Looking at the other women, Starbright saw that they concurred in Wagner's opinion. That was cogent to the mountain man for Wagner had felt the hand of Redburn whereas the others only feared it.

"Till then," said Starbright reluctantly.

"Now, wasn't there talk about a marriage?" said Rita, her gaiety instantly returning.

"Doc, what you waiting on?" yelled Starbright, and he put his arm possessively about her.

And so it was done, on the bank of the River of the West, with only the gorge walls about them but with a clearing sky above. Ralph Wagner, when he had said the words of marriage, clasped the hands of the couple beneath his own hand. When he asked the divine blessing, it was spoken strongly, sincerely, and this was either because of his friendship or because the missionary was at last winning his own peace of mind. That, plus the marriage, settled Dix Starbright in a course of patience, a hard course but one he knew to be wise.

Immediately after the ceremony, he took his bride out onto the river again. The others showed no hurry to break camp. That suited Starbright, for he wanted to get ahead with Rita and keep ahead, and now he cursed the vanished fog that might have given them privacy for another night. But a cold, bright sun had broken through the overcast. Now the immense rises of the palisades were plainly, splendidly visible to them. Instead of frightening Rita they kept her watching in fascination.

Finally he said, "I don't see any chance of getting lost again."

She dimpled. "As every girl does, I've read a lot about weddings. I can't remember a line on how to take a honeymoon in this kind of situation."

"Your dad's got sense," Starbright reflected. "And so's Wagner. Maybe they'll lay over a day."

"If they don't think of it, the women will. Anyhow, it's not far to the valley now."

"A thousand miles and a thousand years."

"Where'll we live?" she asked.

"Homestead. I got to have space and a little wilderness about me. Couldn't stand the kind of thing your dad'll do. That all right?"

"Wonderful, darling. I warn you, I intend to present you with many children."

"Long as you give me a hand in it, that's fine."

All day they ran with the short river reaches plainly visible to them. There was no sign of their being followed by the other raft, yet there was always the chance that it was on the water and not too far behind. Starbright kept watching, and he caught Rita at it, too. But there was an advantage in the cleared weather. He could pick their next camp with care, and as day ran out he began to watch for a place where they could not be come upon as easily as in the preceding camps. He found it, presently, a strip of open beach on the north side with a mountain-locked meadow behind. Starbright put in. Rita leaped lightly ashore to catch the line and snub it to a tree. The instant Starbright followed, she was in his arms.

"For a woman who shot me recently," said Starbright, "you're a friendly little cuss."

"One way to get a husband!" Rita said happily.

"We make camp first?"

"No! We might have company!"

He caught her up and walked into the first real aloneness of their marriage, a place where the thick tree stand had sheltered a springy cushion of needles and old grass from the weather. There Starbright's blanket coat went down and themselves upon it. Her arms would not let go of him, nor her mouth leave off its search for his. "Darling — darling!" And then she had for him more than she had promised, even as she drew from him all that she had sought. "I'm a savage!" she murmured. "And I love it, my man — my man — !"

Twilight pressed down upon their campfire, and the river was still empty of craft. "I like my new papa," said Starbright, dumping a load of firewood at the blaze. "And I like my new friend. That's Doc. You know, Rita, there was a while when I almost went to preaching at him. That's funny, when I never believed in it much, myself."

"I do, Dix. And you do in your heart."

"Not hellfire and brimstone. Not sour-faced piety." Starbright shook his head.

"Of course not. That's not the real thing, at all. What Wagner's got is real."

"Real or not, I'll listen when he talks."

"Still glad you married me, darling?" Rita asked impulsively. "You're not finding it disappointing?"

"Good God A'mighty!" bawled Starbright, and pulled her to him.

But she put him off with a kiss and went on cooking their supper, biscuits in the Dutch oven, bacon in the skillet, coffee on the coals and smoke everywhere. "The night I shot you," recalled Rita, "I died a thousand times. Why must women shoot the men they love?"

"Prudes," Starbright reflected, "do things like that to cover desires that ain't as lady-like."

"You'll have to quit saying 'ain't'," Rita decided. "Not so good in a governor."

"What's that you say?"

"You're going to be Oregon's first governor. Simply because I want to be called Her Excellency. Or would I be?"

"Giddy as can be."

"Certainly. I've got a husband at last."

Night, and they were still alone. Starbright made one bed. Rita said, "I'm sick to death of sleeping in my clothes." When Starbright grinned, she added quickly, "I have night-gowns along. Oh, darn it — they're on the other raft!"

"That gives me no pain. I turn my back while you get to bed?"

She answered by beginning to undress. He followed suit. It was like they had been married for years. She was yeasty, relaxing, and yet with a firm core of decency and courage. His love was greater than his want as he slipped in beside her. For a moment he lay thinking of their hands clasped together under Wagner's while the blessing of God was asked for their union. Thus tenderness came to Starbright, making their intimacy a precious thing, yet a thing possessed of the fires of life that quickly caught them up. . . .

They waited all through the next day for the other raft to come in. The rays of the low autumn sun splashed brightly on the water when finally Starbright glanced up-stream to see that Kelly Lang had detected the smoke of the big fire. Rita, her arm about her husband's waist, said, "We're going to be crowded from here to the valley. But I'll be wanting you, my man."

"You got doubts about me?"

"I'm wondering now how I got out of it

265

those other times." Her voice lost its gaiety. "Dix, remember your promise to Ralph."

"Not to hunt Redburn? I won't. But I can't say I don't itch to meet him."

"I'll die again. Another thousand times. But if I know it's because you have to do it, I can bear it."

The others came in casually, so much so that Starbright had to grin. He walked up to Kelly Lang. "Pop," he announced, "I could kiss you on that sun-burned nose."

"I gave you my daughter for that purpose," said Lang. "But it's nice to know you feel that way, my boy."

"It's your gold," Wagner commented. "He's got the girl, and now he's itching to get his hands on the money."

"On plough handles," Starbright corrected. "It's home-spun for me from here on, and the devil with buckskin."

"Shucks," said Rita. "I was planning to chew up some deer skins and make you a new suit."

The women claimed her, quite as if she had been away on a long honeymoon. Ruby Lafferty, though not yet showing her own delicate condition, was particularly solicitous. Starbright felt proud and fulfilled as he helped the men secure the newly arrived raft for the night's camp. Later, bedded down in the intimate, familiar circle of his friends, his bride sedately beside him, he decided that he could somehow endure the weeks that must pass before there could be further privacy.

Another clear day followed in which the rafts ran on steadily. Now they began to pass other camps on the shore and put in each time to see if help was needed. At last they came to a ferry, operated by an earlier settler, whereby the livestock was put across in order to gain the portage road not now far beyond. There was no need for the rafts to stop at this place, but Starbright put in. He sought the ferryman, a gaunt man in homespun, and described Redburn and Boze.

The man scratched his head. "I been hoppin' ever since the first of your train got this far," he reported. "But I recollect that pair. Alone and with no outfit a'tall. They tried to buy grub from me but I ain't got it to spare. Got tough and took what they wanted."

"That's them," Starbright agreed. "Where are they now?"

"Made me put 'em across. By now they ought to be to Fort Vancouver. Chasin' 'em, bub, or tryin' to steer clear of 'em? Was I you, I'd keep my distance."

"How long ago was it?"

"Four, five days."

This specific report on his enemies rekindled the urgencies in Starbright. Fort Vancouver was not a day's horseback ride below the portage. By now Redburn and Boze could have outfitted themselves and returned to the vicinity of the portage. In another day the rafts would be there, and then — ! Starbright's eyes were aglow as he walked back down to the rafts.

When in resumed rain the rafts ran ashore at the upper end of the portage road, it was like coming upon a crude, sprawling boom town. Tents and wagon sheets had been set up for shelter, many raft parties having reached here ahead of their livestock. Again, spread out wherever pasture was available, were horses and oxen arrived ahead of the rafts they were to meet. The road that climbed into the hills in order to circumvent the rapids was steep and bottomless, a twisting ditch of jelly-like mud. Wagons were stuck along its length, thoroughly clogging the trail.

Starbright's inquiry disclosed that Lafferty had not yet come in. That surprised Starbright and worried him. They, themselves, faced the prospect of being pinned down helpless if they had to wait here too long. He went back to report the news to the party, saying, "We'll make as comfortable a camp as we can. We'll let our rafts down the rapids. After that there's nothing to do but set."

"Think Lafferty had trouble?" Wagner asked, looking narrowly at the trail running east.

"Not unless somebody made it for him. Redburn and Boze are on ahead. The ferryman told me. Lafferty's a good man on any trail, but this is as tough as they come."

"Redburn's ahead?" Wagner asked sharply.

"Or lurkin' somewhere around here."

The others had pulled straight, their faces tightening as they listened. But they had to be warned, and Starbright watched fear leap into Rita's eyes and be put down. He saw her chin lift as her will steeled itself. Her father had raised a hand and started rubbing a cheek.

"I say supper's the important thing, right now," said Mrs. Owen. "You men get our camp set up."

Later, as he strolled restlessly about, Starbright began to sense the despair that weighted the big, stalled camp. The valley of its dreams was only a short way ahead now in terms of distance. Yet the overland trail had led from barrier to barrier, with each more difficult than the one before. Food was running short again, the weather threatened to be bad. Such stock as had come in was weakened by the days on the cattle trail, for it had been hurried along too swiftly to graze. Tempers were short, with quarrels breaking out senselessly and violently. Yet Starbright liked the anger better than the fear he saw in so many eyes. A hot head still had the capacity to fight, while apprehension was the door to disaster.

The next morning Starbright, Lang, and Wagner completely unloaded the rafts. Their camp was on the eastern edge of the big, disheartened aggregation, at a point where they could watch the stock trail for Lafferty and their animals. Since they would need Wagner's wagon for the portage, they set it up and moved it by hand to the camp so that the women could use it to sleep out of the weather. They set up a fly at its side and thus gained extra protection from the now pelting rain. But the underfooting everywhere was sticky enough to pull off a man's boots.

"And now to put the rafts down so they'll be ready and waiting," said Starbright.

"We going to ride them?" Lang asked nervously.

Starbright laughed. "Hell, man, you're getting as jittery as the rest. We've got to rope down — a long, hard job. Me and Doc, that is, for you're going to stay here and defend your gold and Rita in case your almost son-in-law should show himself."

"I've got Owen's rifle," said Mrs. Owen. "It's not likely that man would get his way. If you need Lang, take him along."

"He'd help," Starbright admitted, seeing that Lang wanted to go.

"Mrs. Owen," said Kelly Lang, "I've learned to be blunt and practical on this trail. I tell you now I aspire to marry you before we've been in the valley a winter."

The woman gave Lang a startled glance, then seemed caught in a not unpleasant confusion. Her half smile lingered as she turned hastily to her cooking. Warmth touched Starbright's heart, with the intuitive awareness that it would happen. Perhaps Lang got his answer in that same moment for the man was smiling as they returned to the rafts.

Letting the two rafts down the long rapids proved as difficult as Starbright had estimated. Wild water ran for the length of the wagon portage, at first a series of rapids, then swift and narrow channels too dangerous to navigate. But this was the last barrier in the water passage. Once reloaded below, the rafts could keep going to Fort Vancouver. Those that preferred could put in at the mouth of the Sandy, on the south side, and take an overland trail to Oregon City.

The three men got the crude craft roped down the long reach and tied up in the slack water of the lower river. There Starbright got his first look at the downstream end of the portage operation. One by one the streaming, mud-plastered wagons and teams came lumbering off the hill to the edge of the river. The people accompanying them looked even muddier and worse abused. Women had removed their shoes and stockings and pinned up their skirts to wade in the cold mud. Older children also waded, while the smaller ones had to be lugged all the way.

As each vehicle reached the river, there began a repetition of the scene back at the distant *dalles*. The wagon was emptied of its contents, the wagon-box once more being removed and set aboard the raft and then reloaded — wearing, monotonous, ceaseless toil, with yet another lap of the journey to be faced and undertaken. These people looked worse beat than those at the upper end of the portage.

The physician in Wagner was immediately aroused. As soon as the rafts were tied up, he began to visit the camps scattered far and wide in the dripping timber and even onto the windswept flat. Finally he said, "Dix, you and Kelly go on. I'll stay here a while. These people need encouragement more than pills, but there's something about medicine that gives them a lift."

"Yet they can't be beat," Lang reflected. "They'll go until they drop. Then get up and go again. You're a shepherd of the human spirit, Doc, but I don't agree that the faculty is all to the good. It's got too much durability for the human body and mind. It leads people to kill themselves trying."

"Is that bad?" asked Starbright. "I figure a man's better off dead than whipped."

"I know what it is to be whipped and what it is to be half-dead," Lang said. "I didn't care for either."

Starbright walked on with Lang. They had

gone but a short distance when a settler hustled out to them from a trailside camp. The man said, "Say, Starbright — anybody tell you I caught sight of that Cob Boze yesterday?"

"He had the gall to show himself here?" asked Starbright, frowning.

The settler shook his head, pointing. "He was spyin' on us from up there in the timber. I passed the word around. If he tries it again, he's apt to get shot."

"Thanks, man," said Starbright. They had gone on a few paces before he added to Lang, "Well, you know who Boze was looking for. By now Redburn must know that we've got here."

"We'd better get back to camp!" Lang exploded. He tried to hurry in the mud.

"Take it easy," Starbright advised. "Redburn would rather go up against you and me than Missus Owen."

The big clot of the camp fell behind and forward ran a long, boggy trail that twisted and heaved through the timber. On every reach, at first, they saw wagons, some pulling laboriously forward, others stuck fast. The stream of foot traffic continued. Starbright and Lang gave up trying to protect themselves from the soupy mud.

The two men were within a couple of miles of the upriver camp when, coming to a turn on the downhill grade, they heard the sudden outcries of a woman close ahead of them.

Starbright flung Lang a look and tried to bolt forward but found running to be impossible. They slogged on around the bend to see a wagon in the middle of the road below them. It was halted and two of its oxen were down in the mud. A woman stood beside the vehicle. She began to scream louder as the men came into view. Hysteria, thought Starbright, for there was no one but her, and no sign of any disturbance.

Drawing closer, he saw that her skirts were pinned above the mud that came halfway to her knees. She had both her hands pressed into her abdomen. She kept calling to them to hurry.

"By God, she's having a baby!" bawled Starbright, and now he managed to move faster.

Starbright had a second of sheer panic. He yelled, "Hold on till I move you to the grass!"

"I dassn't move!"

Lang had caught up. Starbright roared, "Throw something out of the wagon I can lay her on!" and grabbed hold of the settler woman. Lang slipped and fell flat in the mud when he tried to grab the tail gate. Then he caught hold and went up. Bundles flew out to splash in the mire, then boxes.

Starbright kicked two boxes together. The woman let out a big groan as he swung her up and splashed across to put her down flat on the wooden surfaces. She still held herself, and as he pulled her hands away the woman let out another moan and went limp.

Starbright acted by instinct from there on. Lang had thrown out blankets, and Starbright covered the woman. She was gasping, giving out little grunts. When he dared to look again, the child had been born.

"You can quit unloading that wagon!" he called to Lang. "It's safe to come out!"

It was a moment before Kelly Lang dared even to look out from behind the wagon sheets. His face was white. "One thing I know!" he breathed. "This part's no fun!"

They let the woman rest a while, and then Starbright said, "It's a boy."

"Is it?" For the first time she smiled. "I'm glad."

"Somebody better go for Doc," Starbright said, concerned again.

"I'll get started," Lang said heartily.

"Whoa, man. I done my turn. You can take over." Without giving Lang a chance to protest, Starbright was off, back over the long and wearisome trail.

He met Ralph Wagner before he had reached the other end. The doctor only smiled at Starbright's breathless news, saying, "See what you're facing?"

"When Rita has young 'uns," Starbright vowed, "I'll keep her away from mudholes.

Come on, Doc. That papoose might of starved to death by now."

"He'll let his mother know when it's dinnertime."

By the time they reached the stalled wagon, the woman's husband had returned. Some women were coming from the other camp, he said, to help. Starbright and Lang were all too glad to go on.

CHAPTER NINETEEN

They reached their own camp to find that Lafferty still had not arrived with the livestock. Ruby had lost control of her emotions and was plainly distressed.

"We'll give him one more day," Starbright told her. "If he don't show by then, I'll scout back and see what happened. You watched what come in on the trail today. You see any stock that left after he did?"

Ruby shook her head. "I questioned every man who came in. Nobody saw him."

"Because he was behind them," Starbright pointed out. "We won't worry yet."

"Oh, won't we?" Ruby retorted.

Darkness came in, Wagner arriving at the camp soon afterward. He reported that the settler had pitched camp where he was, with several others remaining with them. Supper had been kept waiting for the doctor, and now they ate it. They had barely finished when a man came slogging along the trail and turned in to their fire.

The light showed him to be plastered with mud from top to bottom. He said, "They want the doc on the lower end."

"Not again!" Wagner groaned. "What's wrong?"

"They shot a man. That Cob Boze. Simpson, he caught the skunk spyin' again and cut loose. Dropped him."

"Kill him?" Starbright demanded.

"I reckon," the settler drawled. "But not yet. Boze, he's the one yellin' for Doc. Only seemed right and decent I should fetch him. And Boze wants Lang."

"Me?" Lang asked. "Not for a million!"

"Might be worth your while," Starbright told him. "Boze was in with Redburn, and if he's turnin' Christian he might clear your title to that gold."

"The gold isn't worth the walk," Lang said. "But I'll go."

Even though he felt that Lang should go, Starbright felt a stir of uneasiness. He wondered what chance there might be that this settler was somehow helping Redburn to work a ruse in order to draw the two men away from the camp. But the rain-soaked, muddy man had an honest, kindly face and appeared far better suited to the role he had declared — that of a man willing to make the rough hike out of plain human sympathy. Starbright's appraisal eased him as to the possibility of a trick, yet left him somehow disturbed and restless.

Wagner left with Lang with the understanding that they would not try to return before morning. When they had gone, Rita said, "Poor Ralph. That's a taste of what he'll always have practicing medicine on the frontier."

"It gives him something, though," said Starbright. "Something I think he values."

"Dad's found something, too," she reflected. "For the first time in his life he's down to earth, rubbing elbows with plain people and loving it. He's found his element."

"And you?"

Rita smiled. "Yes, but it's going to be a while before I'm in it again."

"Lots of woods," he reminded her.

"And lots of mud."

"Well, you and the other women had best hit the blankets, nice and dry in the wagon. A regular hen house." Starbright sighed regretfully. "What a waste that is."

"And you?" Rita asked, smiling.

"I'll sit up a while."

"You expect Redburn?"

"Sooner or later," said Starbright. "I'd as leave have it sooner."

When the women had all vanished into the wagon, he seated himself under the fly where shadow kept him concealed from everything except the trail and the river, itself. A drizzling rain fell through the firelight, hissing and mixing steam into the smoke. Other fires winked through the trees, sometimes shut off by moving figures, then coming back.

Redburn could not get at this camp from that direction. But the other side was fully exposed, and he could sneak up on that approach. Starbright had protected himself from a shot from that angle, although he doubted that his enemy would operate in a way that would arouse the whole camp. The fellow would need time if he hoped to get away with the gold as well as reap revenge, and Tyre Redburn was a man who would play for the whole pot.

A great while passed in which the other fires grew free of loungers, the raveled sound of distant talk fading away. It was Ruby who broke the long silence, startling Starbright when she thrust her head through the slit in the wagon sheet, excited.

"Isn't that stock coming?" she asked.

Starbright had heard nothing but, keening his ears, he began to detect a heavy, rustling movement in the quieter drone of the rain.

"It is for fair!" he said and shoved to his feet. "And maybe it's your man!"

Although there was only a chance of that, an enormous relief leaped through him. He shoved to a stand and moved down to the trail. It was fifteen minutes before the first livestock of the bunch appeared, shuffling along the trail. Behind were two riders, slumped and all but asleep in the saddle. A third man brought up the rear, sitting his saddle in the same spent, stoical way. None of the men was Lafferty, nor had Starbright recognized the stock. But he stayed where he was, dreading to face Ruby with her lifted hopes and now her disappointment.

The bunch plodded past. Starbright was about to warn them that they had already passed the available pasture, but the hind rider, now abreast of him, pulled down his horse. He had his head tipped forward as if to let the rain run off his hat-brim, and otherwise was bundled to the ears. But as he halted, he raised his head and brought his hand out of his greatcoat pocket. The hand held a pistol and the face that disclosed itself with the lifting head brought a grunt out of Starbright.

"Stand still, man!" drawled Tyre Redburn.

"You cunning devil!" Starbright breathed.

"Shut up."

Redburn didn't stir. He was waiting for the herd and riders to move on ahead. Starbright understood then that the man had used expediency, seeing his chance to fall in behind the all but dead headers and catch his enemy flat-footed. It was smooth and it had worked. Although Ruby undoubtedly was still watching, she seemed not to have become alarmed by what had so far transpired. To her it would appear that Starbright was only questioning this fellow about Lafferty.

Starbright fought down the urge to sound an alarm so violent it would rouse the entire camp and frighten Redburn off. But the gun in Redburn's hand was steady, trained on Starbright's stomach, and he would have time to avenge himself on Rita before he fled.

Softly Starbright said, "You and Boze seem to have spied on different ends of the portage. Likely you don't know that they shot him this evening."

"I don't know why I'd care."

"Loyal as hell, ain't you?"

"I make out."

Patiently Redburn waited for the moving cattle to pull into the forward distance. Then he said, "It would be foolish for any of you to make an outcry. I want the gold, and I want Rita."

"In that order? On the second, you're a little late. We've been married four, five days."

"Married?" For a moment Redburn was wholly silent and unmoving. Then he laughed softly. "All the more reason for me to take her. I'd rather take your wife than your girl."

"Goddamn you!"

"Stand still, Starbright. We're going up to your camp very quietly. You're going to lash the gold to my saddle while I hold this gun on you. We'll try not to rouse the ladies. Except Rita, when I'm ready to go."

"Leaving me dead?"

"Alive, Starbright, to wonder where we are and what we're doing."

Redburn apparently had not guessed that Ruby's worry for her husband had caused her to detect the sound of the moving cattle. Starbright prayed that she was gaining some insight into the situation, would withdraw and warn the other women. That was his hole card, its value uncertain, and his only hopeful course was to obey Redburn until it became impossible.

Using one hand, Redburn swung from his horse. He stepped close to Starbright, extracted his gun, then moved a little back, which from the camp would not present a disturbing appearance. In his quiet voice, he said, "Go on in. If I can't take Rita, I'll kill her. Nothing you can do will save her. Remember that." He tossed Starbright's pistol out into the darkness.

"I remember a lot of things, man," Starbright breathed. "The Pheasant and Liz Templeton among them."

Redburn wasn't listening. He was staring at the hind end of the wagon as they moved closer. Glancing that way, which he had feared to do previously, Starbright's heart skipped a beat. Ruby's head still showed there; she had not divined the meaning of this happening, the night and the situation confusing her as it had Starbright. She simply waited to hear what report there was of her man.

"Quiet, Ruby!" Redburn called softly. "And don't try to duck back! It's me!"

"Redburn!" But Ruby had the discipline to speak only in a shocked whisper.

"Come on out, Ruby," Redburn replied.

The girl slipped through the canvas and descended the wagon steps. She was in her nightgown and barefooted, and as she stepped out into the mud she halted, a small and frightened shape. Her discovery by Redburn had compounded the problem for Starbright. But there still was one faint hope. The fact that they had not aroused to see if Lafferty had got in showed that Rita and the Owen women were soundly asleep. Yet there was a chance that the low talk would disturb one of them, that, listening, someone would gather the situation. Those women had courage, too, and Starbright prayed mutely.

"Now, bring out the gold, Starbright," said Redburn. "Don't try to fool me, and take it easy. Remember that I've got Ruby in front of me now."

"The gold," Starbright announced, "is in the wagon. You don't think we're fools enough to leave it laying around, do you? Not when we've known since we got here that you were laying for us. What are you going to do about that, Redburn?"

"All right," said Redburn. "Rouse the other women. Warn them that Ruby will pay for any indiscretion on their part. Hurry, Starbright."

Starbright went up into the wagon to find that Rita and the two Owen women were still sleeping soundly. He touched Rita's shoulder, whispering, "Quiet — Redburn!" as she came awake. He heard her soft, despairing gasp, then he brought the Owen women awake. "You'll have to go out where he can watch you," he concluded.

"Oh, Dix — Dix — !" Rita sobbed. "Let him have the gold! Who cares?"

"You know there's more than that in his mind. Hurry now! Maybe I'll get my chance."

Thinly clad though they were, the women ducked out into the rain-drenched night, descending to the muddy ground and moving over under the fly with Ruby. Lang's regained gold had been transferred to a small cowhide trunk, which Starbright dragged to the tail gate.

"You're going to have a time managing this, man," he warned Redburn.

"Put the gold in a sack, Starbright, and lash it to my saddle. Rita and I will walk to where I've got other horses."

"Rita and you?" Rita hooted.

"That's right, darling. I hear you're his little wife, now. I trust that you stored up enough treasures in his memory to last a lifetime. That's all he'll ever have of you."

"Have you any idea how loathesome you are, Tyre?"

"Only when somebody has done me dirt, darling. As Starbright did when he took you away from me."

"You're insane!"

"Only when it comes to you, my dear. And gold." Tyre Redburn laughed softly. "Even there I can be extremely brilliant. Ask your husband, darling. I had a gun on him before he even recognized me."

"This trunk's locked," Starbright said. "Kelly Lang's got the key. What are you going to do about that, man?"

Redburn swore. "Then lash the damned trunk to the saddle! And hustle! Edith, you go in and get Rita's clothes so she can dress." Edith Owen moved up into the wagon.

Starbright dragged the trunk down to the ground, its heavy thumping on the steps declaring its great weight. Redburn was desperately reckless in his assumption that he could pack it very far on a wet riding saddle, however carefully tied there. So his spare mounts and pack horses must be close. With Rita his hostage, he would feel safe to take whatever time he needed to make better preparations for whatever trail he proposed to ride from here on. Starbright weighed the advantages of waiting in hopes of jumping Redburn by surprise himself against the chances of making a break here. He could not tolerate the thought of Rita's being in the man's power at all.

He said, "This damned thing's heavy, Redburn. Want me to swing it up while you lash it or the other way around? I can't do both by myself."

"Lift it, man, and quit stalling!"

Redburn led the horse over to where Starbright waited with the small trunk at his feet. As he stopped the animal he swung it so that he still faced Starbright and the watching women. Edith emerged from the wagon at that moment, with clothing over her arm and a pair of shoes in her hand.

Redburn said, "Give that to Rita, then come back here." When the girl had complied, he resumed, "Now, when Starbright lifts that trunk up, you throw the stirrups over the top and tie them together good and tight. I'll check up afterward. You'd better get around on the other side of the horse."

The man was giving Starbright no opening whatsoever. The trunk required his full strength as he lifted it to the saddle seat. Edith threw a stirrup over the top, then came around to repeat with the other. When she had battened down the trunk with the stirrup leathers, which formed a cradle for it, Redburn said, "Now, Starbright, get a light rope and lash the trunk handles to the cinch rings. Snug, man, because if it slips I'll stop right there and collect from Rita."

"Ah, no, Tyre!" Rita called. "And don't move, or I'll drop you!"

Starbright swung as one with Redburn. Rita had a pistol in her hand, and it was leveled on Redburn.

"Where'd you get that?" Redburn thundered.

"It's Owen's. Edith smuggled it out with my clothes. Drop that gun, Tyre. Quick."

Redburn let out an oath. He had been watching the loading, all but disregarding the women. Starbright sensed that he was going to fight, having all to gain or all to lose. His first strike would be at Rita, calculated on the chance that she could not make good on her threat. Starbright moved, though Redburn's gun still covered him, gambling everything on the sudden confusion in the man.

Redburn let out a growl of warning. Once he shot, Rita could drop him, with the firing rousing the whole big camp. As Starbright swung forward, Redburn chose to belt at him with gun barrel and tried to swing the horse between himself and Rita. The gold was loaded, and suddenly he seemed bent on getting away with that alone. Then Starbright was on him in full assault.

They went down in the mud, Starbright using both hands in a frantic effort to wrest the gun from Redburn. The watching women seized the chance to rend the night with screams.

"Goddamn you, Starbright!" Redburn

gasped. "Always in my way! Damn your soul to hell!"

"This time we'll see who goes there!"

Redburn realized that his last chance had been swept away. They rolled, kicking and butting. It was a resumption of that terrible struggle back at Pacific Springs, and Redburn seemed to remember all the weeks in which he had nursed a broken body and a consuming hate.

Though Rita had a gun, she was unable to use it without equal danger to Starbright, who yelled at her to leave it to him. He was vaguely aware of resounding yells from up in the main camp, responding to the women's outcry. But he wanted no help, nothing but to finish this thing himself. He got the gun away from Redburn and batted it aside, but the man gave a mighty heave and came out from under him. Berserk and powered by a wild man's strength, Redburn rolled on top.

He began to beat Starbright's head into the mud as his own had been pounded with such crippling results. But this was not hard, baked desert earth. With a belting, backhand blow, Starbright hit the side of Redburn's head.

It jarred the fellow, and a sudden heave toppled him. Locked together, they rolled almost to the campfire, driving in punches that brought pained grunts from them both.

There they broke apart and scrambled up,

Starbright all but blinded by mud. Reaching down, Redburn grabbed a brand from the fire. He jabbed it at Starbright's face, forcing him back. He kept darting searching glances at the ground, hunting the pistol he had lost. Detecting that fact, Starbright disregarded the brand and bored in again. Redburn struck him across the side of the head with the burning stick, which Starbright seized and wrenched from him. But Starbright disdained its use in retaliation and tossed it away.

There was a general outcry to the west. Men were running down through the timber. But they would leave it to Starbright, for it was a situation in which he would tolerate no help from anybody.

For a moment the two mud-coated, fighting men simply stared at each other, chests heaving, breaths sucking noisily. The trapped desperation had gone from Redburn, bravado replacing it. He had lost his hat but was still clumsily bundled against the weather, as was Starbright.

Softly, Redburn said, "End of the road for me, all right. How about you, Starbright? Want to quit while you're still hanging together?"

"Pull off your coat. Let's finish it."

They stripped bare from the waist up and again confronted each other, a considerable gallery of watchers formed now, tight-faced and silent men aware of the terrible personal struggle being waged within the more general conflict. Even the women, horrified and sickened, watched with hypnotic intentness.

After his long survey, Redburn sprang in as Starbright surged forward to meet him. Freed of excess clothing, both had better command of themselves, better balance and greater freedom of movement. They circled, sparring and driving in, equally matched and equally raging. Starbright's intense concentration defined only the shape of Redburn out of all the images before him, a figure that he meant to destroy forever.

Yet Redburn fought to survive, if only to be hanged, and dredged up all the cunning he possessed. He struck out only when it suited him, the blow jolting Starbright each time. Otherwise he covered himself out of some past experience with boxing that gave him an uncanny skill at guarding against Starbright and deflecting his attacks. Again and again Starbright bored forward to spend himself uselessly and to be driven painfully back. Redburn had not fought this kind of fight at South Pass, and this time he meant to win.

There was an instant in which Redburn rested buttocks and elbows in the mud, head canted back, his sucking breath a tearing noise. Starbright had his chance to go in with his feet the way some mountain men would have done it, using hard heels to stomp the flesh from Redburn's face and the life from his tortured body. Yet something restrained him, the burning need to outlast his enemy and thus prove his supremacy beyond a doubt.

Redburn's courage was breaking. He stiffened his neck and stared upward at Starbright, bewildered, his best delivered and ineffective. He had lost his chance for victory before the eyes of the woman he had coveted, and this stinging blight to his male prowess got him back on his feet. But the punch that had felled him still had him dazed. He lurched as he drove at Starbright, arms outstretched, now trying to close and grapple. Starbright brought a shoulder up and over, arm and fist sledging forth. The fist went numb as its knuckles cracked on the man's jaw, a dull pain climbing the arm.

Yet Redburn had halted in midstride, his back bowing, his extended arms flopping down. Buckling knees let him drop. Unconsciously Starbright lifted his damaged hand and blew on it, watching closely. The gallery pressed in.

Slowly it dawned upon those about it that the inert figure in the churned mud was done forever with the passions and pursuits of the world. Starbright noted the odd misalignment of the man's neck and realized that the warped soul of the man was gone from the once splendid body. Then Starbright walked away.

His knees were weak, and he lurched as he went over to where Rita waited with the other women. Panting, he said, "You all go to some other camp for the rest of the night. You've had enough of this."

"Are you all right, Dix?" Rita asked.

He put a muddy hand on her shoulder and stared down into her intent eyes. "I'm sick to my soul, but I had to do it. It's done, so I'm all right. . . ."

Kelly Lang and Ralph Wagner were back early the next morning. They brought a confession signed by Cob Boze. The man had died during the night, repentant in the way of cravens striving belatedly to make amends because of their fear of the mystery awaiting them beyond death. The confession was hardly needed, except that it gave Lang a clear title to his gold and justified the fates of the two dead men.

By then Starbright's broken hand was swollen and throbbingly painful. There was little the doctor could do except to immobilize it. A while later Lafferty came in with the livestock. The party was thus put in shape to pursue its way on to the Willamette settlements.

But first there was a task so characteristic of the long trail. The settlers had dug a grave on the hill for Tyre Redburn and had sewn his body in a wagon sheet. They spoke to Starbright, who went to Wagner and said, "It's a hard thing to ask, I reckon, Doc. But the people figure that Redburn's entitled to a decent burial. So do I."

Wagner nodded, then said softly, "Once I was bitter. I'd trained a long while for a life in the Western missions. I found it was going to be shockingly different to what I'd dreamed. But I hadn't finished my training, Dix, that was all. The trail finished it for me."

"You going to that mission, Doc?"

Wagner only nodded again, then started off to where they waited for him at the open grave of Redburn.

Starbright looked at his wife and said, "If he can do it, so can we." He nodded toward the group above them.

Rita said, "Yes. He had a lot more to put behind than we have. Come on, darling."

They moved up the wet hill, her hand clasped in his.

ABOUT THE AUTHOR

Chad Merriman was the pseudonym Giff Cheshire used for his first novel, *Blood on the Sun*, published by Fawcett Gold Medal in 1952. He was born in 1905 on a homestead in Cheshire, Oregon. The county was named for his grandfather who had crossed the plains in 1852 by wagon from Tennessee and the homestead was the same one his grandfather had claimed upon his arrival. Cheshire's early life was colored by the atmosphere of the Old West which in the first decade of the century had not yet been modified by the automobile. He attended public schools in Junction City and, following high school, enlisted in the U.S. Marine Corps and saw duty in Central America. In 1929 he came to the Portland area in Oregon and from 1929 to 1943 worked for the U.S. Corps of engineers. By 1944, after moving to Beaverton, Oregon, he found he could make a living writing Western and North-Western short fiction for the magazine market and presently stories under the byline Giff Cheshire began appearing in *Lariat Story Magazine*, *Dime Western*, and *North-West Romances*. His short story 'Strangers in the Evening' won the Zane Grey Award in 1949. Cheshire's Western fiction was characterized from the beginning by a wider historical panorama of the frontier than just cattle ranching and frequently the settings for his later novels are in his native Oregon. *Thunder on the Mountain* (1960) focuses on Chief Joseph and the Nez Perce war, while *Wenatchee Bend* (1966) and *A Mighty Big River* (1967) are among his best-known titles. However, his Chad Merriman novels for Fawcett Gold Medal remain among his most popular works, notable for their complex characters, expert pacing, and authentic backgrounds.